Diana L. Ruzicka

C000221699

Redemptive Suffering in the Life of the Church

Offering Up Your Daily Suffering to Cooperate with Christ in Redeeming the World

Diana L. Ruzicka Publisher
New Market, Alabama

BOOKS ALSO BY DIANA L. RUZICKA
The Descendants of Abbegail (Kallahan) and Felix
Locklin Prunty, 1791-2001.

The Prunty Family Records, 2nd edition, 1987.

CHAPTERS AUTHORED OR CO-AUTHORED
Benefits of Proper Pain Management. In St. Marie, B. (ed). Core
Curriculum for Pain Management Nursing, 2008.

Cancer Pain Management. In Gates, R. & Fink, R. (eds.).
Oncology Nursing Secrets, 3rded, 2008

Economic Issues & Addiction,
In Pain Management Nursing Certification Exam, 2005.

*Patient/Family Education & Counseling, Crisis Management,
Evaluation of Understanding/ Comprehension/Competency,*
In Guide for the Pain Management Nursing Review Course,
American Society of Pain Management Nurse, 2004.

*VHA/DoD Clinical Practice Guideline for the Management of
Post Operative Pain* (Version 1.1). Office of Performance and
Quality, Veterans Health Administration, Washington, DC &
Quality Management Directorate, U.S. Army Medical Command,
July 2001.

Cancer Pain Management. In Gates, R. & Fink, R. (eds.).
Oncology Nursing Secrets, 2nded, 2001

Care of the Patient Receiving Epidural Analgesia module
produced by Pain Management Service, Tripler Army
Medical Center, June 1997.

Cancer Pain Management. In Gates, R. & Fink, R. (eds.).
Oncology Nursing Secrets, 1997.

SELECTED ARTICLE(S)
*Implementing a Pain Management Service at an Army
Medical Center.* Military Medicine, 2001

*To Alan Ruzicka who has supported me
throughout my career,
retirement from the military
and now as I complete a MA in Theology.
To my faithful friend through 30+ years of marriage.*

*To Sister Maria Paulina Sterling, Archdiocese of Chicago,
who demonstrates redemptive suffering in her daily life.
Thank you Sister Maria Paulina for your faithful example.
May the Apostolate of Redemptive Suffering
you are forming be successful.*

*To Betty (1954-2012) & Darrel Kaiser who welcomed
me into their intimate relationship
into the school of suffering as
Betty journeyed through illness, suffering and death.*

Diana Ruzicka, RN, CNS-BC, MSN, MA, MA is a cradle Catholic. She is the third of six children and was born in Manchester, Tennessee and raised in Sunnyvale, California. She served twenty-five years in the United States Army as a registered nurse retiring with the rank of Colonel in 2008. During that time she received a Master in Nursing from Vanderbilt University in Oncology and Nursing Administration. In collaboration with the Chief, Anesthesia Service, Department of Nursing, Department of Surgery and many other departments of the medical center, with a team of five nurses, she started and coordinated a Pain Management Service at Tripler Army Medical Center. There she taught Cancer Pain Management in the Internal Medicine Residency Program and the basics of pain management in the Nursing Anesthesia, OB/GYN Nursing, Hospital Nursing Orientation Programs and to medical department/service staff throughout the medical center. She served on the VA/DoD working groups to develop Post Operative Pain Guidelines and Chronic Opioid Therapy Guidelines. She also holds a Masters in Strategic Studies from the Army War College and a MA in Theology from Catholic Distance University. While on active duty she received the Army Surgeon General's 9A designator for her expertise in Medical Surgical Nursing. Following retirement she was recognized at the Vanderbilt University centennial anniversary celebration as one of the 100 honored graduates. She is a member of the National Association of Catholic Nurses (NACN-USA), The International Catholic Committee of Nurses and Medico-Social Assistants (CICIAMS), Catholic Medical Association, National Catholic Bioethics Center, Army Nurse Corps Association and a reviewer for Pain Management Nursing, the journal of the American Society for Pain Management Nursing. This documents is an edited version of her MA Thesis.

*Now I rejoice in my sufferings for your sake and
in my flesh I complete what is lacking in Christ's afflictions
for the sake of His body, that is, the Church.*
Colossians 1:24

This may be a wicked age, but your lives should redeem it.
Ephesians 5:16

*Suffering does not come into our lives without
the permission or will of the Father*
Mother M. Angelica

*Rejoice in hope, be patient in tribulation, be constant in prayer
Bless those who persecute you; bless and do not curse them.*
Romans 12:12 & 14

*I have said this to you, that in Me you may have peace.
In the world you have tribulation; but be of good cheer,
I have overcome the world.*
John 16:33

*Suffering exists in the world in order to unleash love in the
caregiver.*

Pope St. John Paul II

*Prayer takes on extraordinary power to win graces
For the one praying and for all mankind
When it is united with patient suffering*
Pope St. John Paul II

Sacred Heart of Jesus, I give myself to You.
Navy Admiral Jeremiah Denton

Copyright © 2015 by Diana L. Ruzicka
All rights reserved.
This book and all portion thereof may be reproduced
and used with the permission of the author.
ISBN: 978-0-9710075-1-2

Diana L. Ruzicka Publisher
185 River Walk Trail, New Market, AL 35761
Telephone: 256-852-5519
Email DianaRuzicka53@aol.com

ISBN 978-0-9710075-1-2
90000
9 780971 007512

PREFACE

This paper addresses the concept and practice of
redemptive suffering while chronicling the life and death of a
friend who, with her husband of forty years, allowed me to
accompany her on her end-of-life journey and first hand
understand the value of suffering and observe its redeeming
effect. It refutes neither the Just War Theory of St Augustine nor
the right for a Christian to respond with righteous anger. Jesus
was a carpenter, however the only tool that the Gospels mention
that He fashioned was a whip with which He drove the money
changers from the temple (Jn 2:13-17). Just as suffering and
happiness are not mutually exclusive, practicing redemptive
suffering and protection of person, family and property are not
contradictory. Clausewitz (1780-1831), the Prussian general and
military theorist, says that war is merely the continuation of
policy (politics) by other means.[1] As a woman who served in the
U.S. Army for over 25 years, I disagree with his statement. I
believe that, "War is when politics fail." So, though I do believe
there is a time for war (Ecl 3:8), I believe that we should try our
utmost to resolve conflict through dialogue. To delve into this
further would be another paper. Suffice it to say that nothing in
this paper should be taken to mandate a life of passivity --- unless
that is the life, or action in a particular instance, to which the
Holy Spirit calls a person.

It is also not the intent of the author that people should neglect their health or the suffering of others in order to practice redemptive suffering. These are also not mutually exclusive. There is enough suffering in our everyday life that a person undergoing treatment for a painful condition, should <u>appropriately</u> treat their pain and would still experience plenty of suffering which could be offered up in their daily life. The Stoic approach to suffering is to stifle the complaint. The Buddhist approach to suffering is to suppress the desire.[2] The Christian approach has nothing to do with negation and emptiness. The Christian approach is to take up the cross and be glad to be accounted worthy to suffer for Christ (Mt. 16:24, 1Cor 1:23; Gal 6:14, Acts 5:41).[3] This may be scary at first thought but do continue to read on.

As Christians we are called to alleviate the suffering of others. It is this author's belief that: 1) a key ethical principle, upon which civilized societies are based, is that the ends do not justify the means. We may not do evil so that good may become of it, 2) all human beings are created in the image and likeness of God and have an inherent dignity and inalienable rights to life, liberty (freedom) and property and therefore, 3) the intentional killing of another human being through abortion, infanticide, over-medication or euthanasia in the name of relieving suffering constitute behaviors that cause the actor to sink below what it means to be human. Pope Benedict XVI articulated this best in his recent encyclical *Spe Salvi (On Christian Hope):* "A society unable to accept its suffering members and incapable of helping to share their suffering and to bear it inwardly through "compassion" is a cruel and inhuman society." (SS 38)   Finally, a heresy can be an out and out falsehood, but in most cases a heresy is when a piece of the truth is conveyed as the whole truth (e.g. faith vs. works, Scripture vs. Tradition, joy or happiness vs. suffering etc.). The author believes that joy or happiness can coexist with suffering. These are not mutually exclusive concepts. Please join me in my quest to understand value of redemptive suffering in the life of the Church and how uniting ones suffering by an act of the will in love with the sufferings of Christ's can bring great grace, peace and joy and serve to participate with Christ in redeeming the world.

I wrote on this topic for my theology master's thesis because, though I advocated for appropriate pain management during my career, I regretted to see the effect of over judicious and inappropriate use of morphine when other modalities that targeted the cause of the pain would be more effective. As I neared the time to write my thesis multiple people approached me with stories of their loved ones dying without receiving food or fluids. For some the lack of nutrition and hydration occurred over a several week period in opposition to the desires of the family. During a trip to accompany ill and injured to the Sanctuary at Lourdes, Frances where Mary appeared to Bernadette Soubirous in 1858, I heard of and then met a religious sister who wanted to form a religious order or an apostolate to help people prepare for end-of-life decisions. We prepare for our financial future, we should also prepare for our end-of-life care and decisions. Throughout my career I have asked the family members of individuals who have died if they had a spiritual experienced with their relative. Many shared awe inspiring stories. I began noticing, however, that those who gave morphine to the relatives when their relative was not in pain would report, "No, but she/he died comfortably." God is the author of life and man has no right to take another life. I sincerely worry, that by over medicating individuals at the end of their life and/or withholding food and fluids, we may be interfering with the disposition of a person's eternal soul.

Additionally, if we intentionally kill our babies, infirmed and elderly, our society will lose compassion. I was also intrigued by St. Paul's statement to the Colossians (Col 1:24). What was this that St. Paul was doing with his suffering… for the sake of the Church? Finally I was blessed to accompany Betty and Darrel on Betty's end-of-life journey and was compelled, with Darrel's permission and encouragement, to share their story.

I would like to end the Preface with a special thanks to my sister, Debbie Prunty, for her painstaking review of this document. Her editorial changes and insights are much appreciated. Any errors that remain were my oversight.

ABBREVIATIONS

LE   *Laborem Excerens* (On Human Work)

NG   Nasogastric Tube

PEG   Percutaneous Endoscopic Gastrostomy Tube

SD   *Salvifici Doloris* (On the Christian Meaning of Human Suffering)

SS   *Salve Spe* (On Christian Hope)

GLOSSARY

IV (Intravenous) – A thin, plastic tube inserted into the vein through which fluids are infused to maintain fluid balance, replace fluid losses and treat electrolyte imbalances.

NG Tube – A thin, plastic tube inserted through the nostril, down the esophagus, and into the stomach through with caregivers can deliver food and medicine directly into the stomach.

Opioid Analgesics – Morphine, Dilaudid, Fentanyl (Duragesic Patch), Oxycodone (Oxycontin, Percocet), Demerol etc.

Paracentesis – The perforation of a cavity of the body (e.g. the abdomen) with a hollow needle to remove fluid or gas.

PEG Tube – A tube passed into a patient's stomach through the abdominal wall, most commonly to provide a means of feeding when oral intake is not adequate (for example, because of difficulty swallowing, sedation, ALS disease).

Strontium-89 – A pure beta-emitting radioisotope which targets diffuse bone metastasis in certain cancers. A feasible, safe, effective, well tolerated and cost effective palliative treatment in patients with refractory bone pain which does not cause sedation.[4]

CONTENTS

INTRODUCTION & Betty's Suffering, Part 1 15

I. SUFFERING VERSES PAIN 17

II. THE OLD TESTAMENT, EVIL & SUFFERING 23

III. THE ORIGIN OF SUFFERING – THE FALL 30

IV. JESUS CHRIST AND SUFFERING 39

V. EFFECTS OF CHRIST'S REDEMPTIVE SUFFERING 42

VI. BETTY'S SUFFERING – PART 2 46

VII. THE NEW TESTAMENT AND REDEMPTIVE SUFFERING 48

Christians Will Suffer 48

Suffering for Self and Others 49

How to Respond to Suffering 51

VIII. BETTY'S SUFFERING – PART 3 55

IX. THE NEW TESTAMENT – COLOSSIANS 1:24 58

Rejoicing in Suffering 58

The Suffering of St. Paul 60

Complete what is lacking 61

Suffering for Others 64

X. TWO POPES DESCRIBE HOW TO SUFFER REDEMPTIVELY 67

XI. EFFECTS OF REDEMPTIVE SUFFERING 69

XII. MODERN EXAMPLES OF REDEMPTIVE SUFFERING 73

XIII. BETTY'S SUFFERING – PART 4 79

XIV. DEATH OF A FATHER AND FATHER-IN-LAW 82

CONCLUSION 84

BIBLIOGRAPHY 86

APPENDICES 93

APPENDIX A-MOTHER TERESA OF CALCUTTA 93

APPENDIX B-HELPING JESUS CARRY THE CROSS FROM BETTY BLAND 94

APPENDIX C-ADMIRAL JEREMIAH DENTON, POW, VIETNAM .. 96

APPENDIX D-*IS CHRISTIANITY EASY?* VENERABLE ARCHBISHOP FULTON SHEEN 100

APPENDIX E-*THE PROBLEM OF LOVE*, VENERABLE ARCHBISHOP FULTON SHEEN 104

APPENDIX F-PERSONAL NARRATIVE FROM SHELBY BROWN .. 111

REFERENCES 114

REFERENCE 1 – RESPONSES TO CERTAIN QUESTIONS OF THE UNITED STATES CONFERENCE OF CATHOLIC BISHOPS (USCCB) CONCERNING ARTIFICIAL NUTRITION AND HYDRATION 114

REFERENCE 2 – DECLARATION ON EUTHANASIA 116

REFERENCE 3 – PAPAL DOCUMENTS 125

REFERENCE 4 – CONGREGATION FOR THE DOCTRINE OF THE FAITH (CDF) DOCUMENTS 126

REFERENCE 5 – FREE CONSULTATION ON BIOETHICAL ISSUES 128

ENDNOTES 129

ILLUSTRATIONS

FIGURES

1 – OUR GIFTED HUMAN NATURE 31

TABLES

1 – TYPES OF SUFFERING 27

2 – BRIEF OVERVIEW OF THE FALL & REDEMPTION 36

3 – ISAIAH 53:2-6 – CHRIST'S REDEMPTIVE SUFFERING 41

3 – INSIGHTS FROM THE SCHOOL OF SUFFERING 81

INTRODUCTION & Betty's Suffering, Part 1

In 2012 Betty Kaiser died from pancreatic cancer. While in the acute care hospital, Betty was given a large dose of medication, presumably morphine or another opioid analgesic, which caused her to sleep for 15 hours. Her husband was irate at having 15 hours of the little time he had left with his wife taken away from him. He ordered the hospital staff not to give her any medication without first speaking with him. When she awoke, Betty asked her husband to take her home saying, "They are trying to kill me." Against the physician's wishes, at the insistence of her husband, she was discharged home. Unfortunately Betty would not return to the acute care hospital again. Though she might have benefited from a paracentesis, a procedure to remove fluid from her abdomen, she feared that she would not come out alive.

In the American society today pain and suffering have little value and are to be relieved at all cost. In fact some do not differentiate between pain and suffering. Instead of giving analgesics to relieve physical pain which is their purpose, morphine is administered to people who are not having physical pain in order to hasten their death and reportedly to ease their suffering. The author observed this in at least two recent instances and Appendix E describes a third. "Assisted suicide" and "euthanasia" are now called, "mercy killing: or "alleviating suffering." One home health nursing supervisor told a student nurse that "it takes about a year to turn new nurses around" (to euthanize patients). Several states have legalized euthanasia. A form of 'stealth euthanasia' is being practiced in many hospitals by the denial of food and fluids, treating the pain and discomfort that accompanies hunger and dehydration with escalating doses of morphine and stopping beneficial medications such as insulin and medications which control congestive heart failure or treat infection.[5]

Should the relief of suffering through the use of opioid analgesics regardless of the cause of the suffering be our goal? Is there a value in suffering? Can something be learned from suffering? After examining the concept of suffering and briefly describing several types of suffering, this paper will delve into the meaning and mystery of a particular type of suffering called redemptive suffering. Woven throughout the paper will be the author's personal experience with the recent death of a friend. The final section will describe some personal experiences of saints, a church leader and a Protestant friend.

I

"There is nothing more tragic in all the world than wasted pain. Think of how much suffering there is in hospitals, among the poor, and the bereaved. Think also of how much of that suffering goes to waste!"
Venerable Archbishop Fulton Sheen[6]

Suffering verses Pain

Suffering, when offered up by an act of the will with love in union with the suffering of Jesus Christ in His passion and death on the cross, has both natural and supernatural effects that serve to redeem ourselves and others and built up the Body of Christ. Before we delve into the specifics of this special type of suffering, called redemptive suffering, we will first explore the concept of suffering, differentiate it from pain and evil and provide an overview of its origin looking at both the fall and redemption.

Suffer comes from the Vulgar Latin "sufferie" and from the Latin "sufferre" which can be divided into "sub" = up and "ferre" = to bear. To suffer is to experience pain, illness or injury; to experience something unpleasant (such as defeat, loss or damage; to become worse because of being badly affected by something). In our humanity, as embodied spirits or ensouled bodies, we experience both physical pain and psychological suffering which are intricately intertwined. The nursing profession, which is one of the professions charged with the care of the suffering, differentiates between physical suffering (pain) and psychological or spiritual suffering (suffering). The International Association for the Study of Pain (IASP) defines pain as, "an unpleasant sensory and emotional experience associated with actual or potential tissue damage or described in terms of such damage."[7] Pain has an underlying, although not always objectively measurable, physiological basis which may respond to medication. In 1968 Margo McCaffery, an expert in the field of pain management first defined "pain" as "whatever the experiencing person says it is, existing whenever he or she says it does."[8] This definition acknowledged that though pain has a physiological component, it is always a subjective experience of the person experiencing it.

Suffering by contrast is "a state of severe distress induced by the loss of the intactness of person, or by a threat that the person believes will result in the loss of his or her intactness"[9] Thus, a person could be in pain, for instance labor pains prior to the delivery of a baby, but not be suffering. A person awaiting a cancer diagnosis could conceivably not be in pain but be suffering due to the threat to their person that the cancer diagnosis poses. What will their husband do when they die? Who will take care of him? Will their pain be relieved?

This differentiation is important because the treatment of pain involves the use of various medications and nonpharmacological modalities (e.g. TENS, heat, cold etc.) while the treatment of suffering involves cognitive, behavioral, spiritual and other supportive therapies. Why would this differentiation be important for this paper? Today in many instances in the healthcare arena pain, suffering and something called "air hunger," whose definition has been expanded considerably in recent years, are all being treated with opioid analgesics. The ethical principle of double effect allows "palliative" or appropriate doses of medication like morphine to be administered even if it hasten death --- provided that the goal is not to hasten death and the medication is appropriately used. In many instances, morphine is now being used to alleviate the suffering of family members exhausted from caring for their loved one, for individuals who are experiencing normal changes in breathing patterns due to approaching death erroneously labeled "air hunger," for those suffering but not in physical pain, in doses that far exceed that required to relieve the pain that is present, and erroneously when another more effective treatment is indicated to treat the underlying cause of the pain. Administration of these large doses of opioids may also be due to early entry into terminal care with hospice resulting in the unavailability of specialized and targeted pain treatments (e.g. strontium 89 for metastatic breast or prostate cancer, celiac plexus block for pancreatic and other abdominal cancers, paracentesis to remove fluid from the abdomen causing pressure and pain, etc.) due to cost.

Why is it wrong to intentionally hasten ones death with opioid analgesics? First God is the author of life. Second a society that kills its most vulnerable will lose compassion which is the ability to "suffer with." On a practical level, persons who are overmedicated are unable to communicate with their family members and resolve unresolved issues and say their last goodbyes to those close to them. In my experience working with dying people, there is a "normal" change in their breathing pattern called Cheyne Stokes breathing --- this is not air hunger and does not require the treatment with morphine or other opioids. In the dying trajectory, the person suddenly awakes and says something very clearly or sees a light or others who have passed before. Through this shared experience the living get a glimpse of life on the other side. Sometimes family members believe the person is getting better but then suddenly they lose consciousness again and stop breathing.

Though no one has come back to share their experience, the weeks, days, hours and moments up until death may be one last chance for people to choose for or against God. Over medicating and hastening deaths robs a person of this opportunity for salutatory repentance.[10] Perhaps this is one of the messages of the parable of the laborers in the vineyard in that the landowner (God) paid the same wages to those who labored all day and also to those who worked only the last hour (Mt. 20:1-16). Perhaps even if we accept Christ at the last hour, we have an opportunity for eternal salvation. Our time here on earth, up until the moment of death is precious.

The preceding section examined the concepts of pain and suffering and addressed the medical definitions differentiating suffering (psychological suffering) from pain (physical suffering). Suffering must be differentiated from pain because the care and treatment of each is different. Both types of suffering can be redemptive. However, if inappropriately treated or over-medicated with opioids resulting in the individual's demise the opportunity to obtain redemptive value from suffering is lost and this action could affect the disposition of the person's soul. It is outside the scope of this paper, however, to delineate the various options for appropriate pain management. The specific modalities selected should be based upon the assessment of and the cause of the pain. Appropriate analgesic use does not result in over-sedation of the person --- an adaptation to the sedative effect of opioids should occur in three days to a week. Towards the end-of-life other physiological issues may gradually cause sedation. The treatment of psychological suffering is not opioid analgesics. Finally, many hospices provide excellent end-of-life care. However, a family or person may prefer the assistance of a nursing home, home health care or a palliative care service if they desired care over and above what hospice may cover (e.g. IV hydration, NG tube or PEG tube feeding, parenteral nutrition, paracentesis, nerve block and other specialized pain treatments etc.). This paper will now get back on topic and explore suffering as described in the Old Testament Book of Job specifically looking at the relationship between suffering and evil.

II

"Naked I came from my mother's womb, and naked shall I return; the Lord gave and the Lord has taken away; blessed be the name of the Lord." Job 1:21

The Old Testament, Evil & Suffering

In the Old Testament, suffering was equated with evil. Evil, sin, death and suffering are metaphysically linked (SD 14). Pope St. John Paul II describes this in his Apostolic Letter *Salvifici Doloris* (*On the Christian Meaning of Human Suffering*):

> It can be said that man suffers whenever *he experiences any kind of evil.* In the vocabulary of the Old Testament, suffering and evil are identified with each other. In fact, that vocabulary did not have a specific word to indicate "suffering." Thus it defined as "evil" everything that was suffering. Only the Greek language, and together with it the New Testament (and the Greek translations of the Old Testament), use the verb * = "I am affected by .... I experience a feeling, I suffer"; and, thanks to this verb, suffering is no longer directly identifiable with (objective) evil, but expresses a situation in which man experiences evil and in doing so becomes the subject of suffering (SD 7).

Suffering, whether it be physical or psychological, is an evil. According to St. Augustine, evil is the absence of good.[11] As he contemplated the origin and essence of evil, St. Augustine came to understand that man will suffer or experience evil to a greater or lesser degree throughout his life until he is united with his ultimate good which is God: *"Thou madest us for Thyself, and our heart is restless until it repose in Thee."*[12] Dr. Peter Kreeft defines three basic kinds of evil: suffering, death and sin. "1) Suffering is a disharmony or alienation between ourselves as embodied creatures and something in this physical world. 2) Death is the disharmony, alienation or separation between the soul and the body. And (3) sin is the disharmony or alienation between the soul and God."[13] These evils, suffering, sin and death, entered the world as a result of the fall of Adam and Eve which is explained in the next section.

Returning to the relationship between suffering and evil, it was not until the Jewish Scriptures were translated into to Greek, within a few hundred years of the incarnation and redemption, that man was able to express suffering as an "experienced evil." No longer was the man born blind guilty of an evil as evidenced by his infirmity. The man born blind and the man with the withered hand experienced an evil, experienced suffering, and their fellow man should help relieve this suffering, even on the sacred day of rest, the Sabbath (Mt. 12: 10-13; Mk 3:1-5; Lk 6:6-8).

In the Old Testament, the Book of Job is a sentinel exploration of the meaning of suffering. In the ENDOW study of a Doctor of the Church, St. Catherine of Siena, the authors outline the dialog between Job and God and explore the mystery of Job's suffering.

> Job, a righteous man loses his children, his property, possessions, his health and finally his wife. Job's three friends conclude that his suffering is a result of sin (Job 4:1-27), that God is just (Job 8:1-22) and Job's guilt deserves punishment (Job 11:1-20). These friends, however, are wrong. Job knows that he is a righteous man. He is not evil. The book concludes with Job acknowledging that suffering is within the plan of God and that Job cannot comprehend the full breath of this plan (Job 38:1-42:6). In his case, the evil that befell Job, the suffering he experienced, was not a punishment, instead, it was a trial, a test of Job's righteousness (Job 1:6-12).

> Through this difficult time, God wants Job to recognize that even the just suffer here on earth, and that these sufferings are one way of testing our fidelity. Nevertheless, we must remember that heaven is our true home, and in heaven the just will reap their reward. Most importantly, God teaches Job that as human beings our finite minds cannot comprehend the Divine presence that governs the world.

> Consequently, the problems that we encounter in life must be understood through a broader and deeper awareness of God's providential power, His presence and His Divine wisdom. In Job's case, through his time of trial, the relationship he enjoys with God becomes deeper and stronger.[14]

We learn from the Book of Job that not all suffering is a consequence of or punishment for individual sin. In Job's instance his suffering and loss was a test of a righteous man. God allowed the suffering in Job's life. This allowed Job to know the strength of his faith. Even though Job was a righteous and faithful man, he still questioned God. He cried out. He asked his friend why. A righteous person can ask God why. However, a righteous person remains faithful as exemplified by Job's famous words in the beginning of the book after Job had lost his property and children, "The Lord gave and the Lord has taken away, blessed be the name of the Lord" (Job 1:21).

In Job's suffering Pope Benedict XVI also sees a foreshadowing of Christ's redemptive suffering: "Job's sufferings serve to justify man. By his faith, proved through suffering, he restores man's honor. Job's sufferings are thus by anticipation sufferings in communion with Christ, who restores the honor of us all before God even amid the deepest darkness."[15]

Mother Angelica calls the type of suffering experienced by Job "Witness Suffering." In her booklet, "*The Healing Power of Suffering,*" Mother Angelica describes eight types of suffering: preventive, corrective, repentant, redemptive, witness, interior, personal and wasted. Table 1 lists and defines each type of suffering and provides examples, recommended response and some Biblical references. Witness suffering edifies our neighbor and encourages him to take up his own cross and follow Jesus as he observes another's faithfulness through suffering. On the other hand, redemptive suffering helps our neighbor by carrying his burden and ours.[16] As we will see, all types of suffering can become redemptive when united with Christ's suffering in love and offered for the other by an act of the will.

In summary, it was only when the Bible was translated into Greek as early as the late 2nd century B.C. that the concepts of evil and suffering were able to be separately described. Job's suffering is "experienced evil." Job experiences suffering not as a punishment but as a trial. His suffering also foreshadows Christ's redemptive suffering. Next we will discuss the fall through which suffering, sin and death entered the world followed by Christ's suffering upon which our redemption and cooperation in redemptive suffering is based.

Table 1. Types of Suffering

Definition	Examples	Response
Preventive Prevents us from making errors in judgment, committing sin, becoming worldly, proud and self indulgent	...suffer loss of car keys, delayed departure, missed an accident ...suffer illness, unable to depart, greater sharing of the Gospel in present locale (St. Paul in Galatia) ...chronic illness or bodily suffering prevents sin, boasting, pride ...disappointment, uncertainty & frustration show the right path	Remain close to God and humble Fix on God's mercy & love *Becomes redemptive when we unite this suffering to the sufferings of Jesus* *Sickness has often been the only reason man does not lead a life totally alienated from God.*
Gal 4:14; 1 Peter 4:1-3; Acts 9:23-25; 2 Cor 11:32, 33 & 12:7		
Redemptive To set-free our neighbor free.	...St. Paul's suffering to bring the Gospel ...Any suffering we "offer up"	Offer up our suffering with Jesus' suffering in love for our neighbor so as to build up the body of Christ
2 Cor 1:5,6; Col 2:1, 24 ; Rom 9:2-4		

Definition	Examples	Response
Corrective Purifies the very weakness that produced it	...suffering experienced from disobedience to God's will ...suffering experienced when soul sees the disparity between itself & Jesus ....response of one's' conscience ...neighbor's faults bring out the weak points in our own character & force us to practice virtue	Realization can either change the soul for good or discourage it If we crucify our own self-indulgent passions & desires, we experience freedom as God's sons & daughters
Heb 12:5-7; Rom 7:14-23 & Gal 2:20; John 15:2; Gal 5:22-24		
Interior Suffering within the soul (spiritual or mental pain)	...remembrance of past sorrows, being misunderstood ...fear of failure or boredom ...Resentment, doubts, lukewarmness ....Mother Teresa – thirsting for God but deprived of his presence (dryness) ...mental anguish, doubt, anxiety, worry, discouragement, uncertainty, disappointment	Bear suffering with love & cheerfully acknowledge our weakness. Ok to look up to God with fear & frustration Change personality & temperament slowly by cooperating with God's grace which has the power to change us so as to reflect the person of Christ
Biblical Example		
Repentant The sorrow/ suffering that follows having fallen deeply from grace & realizing God's love	...King David following adultery ...Peter following denial of Jesus ...Paul following his conversion ...Any one of our sins	Realize the sin, recognize it offends God & the community & experience deep sorrow, seek forgiveness in love for God→joy & gratitude, enables us to begin anew and makes us prayerfully vigilant
Mt. 5:5; Psalm 50		
Personal Suffering peculiar to an individual's age, temperament & personality	...colic, growing pain, after 40 spread, age related fears ...nervousness, sensitivity, angry ...James suffered from zeal for the old covenant ...Paul suffered from enthusiasm for the new covenant	...run away from & deny, alcohol, ignore faults Recognize that our reactions not only tell us what faults we possess but their degree of intensity (p25) Admit & listen to voice of God in our soul
Rom 7:21		

Definition	Examples	Response
Wasted Suffering which is to no avail because it is not suffered with love	Suffering experienced by those who expelled the disciples from the synagogues who never knew God …Pharisees suffering with misguided zeal & jealousy Trials & pains received with bitterness and pride	Suffer for and with the love of God in our hearts: lose hope, discouraged, run away, rebel, bitterness & pride
Biblical Example: 1 Cor 13:3; Mt. 6:1; Jn 16:2-3; Acts 7:54		
Witness Suffering that shows that we are servants of God. Our example makes our neighbor desire virtue in his life	…..St. Paul was flogged, sent to prison, mobbed, etc. and he continued to be a servant of God in continuing to preach the Gospel and exhibit virtues. …Calamities seem to befall us and we maintain faith & hope.	Exhibit fortitude (& other virtues) in times of suffering; Maintain our Christian disposition: 1) never worry about tomorrow, 2) be satisfied with our daily bread, 3) seek first the kingdom, 4) be poor, meek, gentle of heart, & 5) dance for joy when abused for His sake
2 Cor 6:4-10		

[1]Source: Mother M. Angelica. *The Healing Power of Suffering.* Irondale, ETWN Catholic Publisher, 1977.

III

I will put enmities between thee and the woman,
and thy seed and her seed:
she shall crush thy head,
and thou shalt lie in wait for her heel.
Genesis 3:15 (Douay Rheims Version)

The Origin of Suffering – The Fall

God made man in His image and likeness and before the
fall man did not experience pain or suffering. He was created
with the preternatural gifts of bodily immortality, integrity
(absence of concupiscence resulting in impassibility) and science
(infused knowledge).[17] He would live forever. He had integrity
which means that his faculties (e.g. intellect, will, passions and
appetites) were fully integrated and functioned optimally. The
intellect sought the truth and informed the will as such. The will
chose the good. The intellect and will governed the passions and
appetites. Though his body was capable of feeling pain and
suffering, the perfect agreement of the body and emotions to the
soul precluded this (impassibility). Finally Adam's knowledge
was infused. It was not acquired in the natural sense of cognition
derived from experience and the reasoning process.[18] See Figure
1 for a diagram of the anthropology of the human person entitled
"Our Gifted Human Nature." When man disobeyed God, he lost
the preternatural gifts. He ruptured his relationship with God,

Figure 1 - **Our Gifted Human Nature**

Faith and reason are like two wings on which the human spirit rises to the contemplation of truth; and God has placed in the human heart a desire to know the truth—in a word, to know Himself—so that, by knowing and loving God, men and women may also come to the fullness of truth about themselves
Fides et Ratio (On the Relationship between Faith & Reason), JPII, 14Sep98

Reason
Philosophy

Faith
Theology

Intellect
(Speculative Intellect)
Oriented towards the truth
Object: God who is true being
Perfected by: Faith
Completely fulfilled in the beatific vision
Truth=correspondence of judgment w/ reality.
Strengthened by Sacrament of the Eucharist

Imagination
Apprehends the likeness of corporeal things even in the absence of the things of which they bear the likeness

Will
Oriented towards choosing good
Perfected by: Charity (by doing what is good)
Based on the power of freedom
Satisfied in the state of beatitude
Strengthened by Sacrament of the Eucharist

Memory
Perfected by: Hope
Purified by the Sacrament of Reconciliation. The way in which the soul has access to reality; being itself; thesaurus, storehouse of being for the soul

Faculties (Capacities)

Conscience
(Practical Intellect)
The act by which the individual judges the objective rightness or wrongness of an act. Object is the good. The good is that which is in accord with the nature of the thing; Perfected by: Good habits & virtues

Heart:
Where the person decides for or against God; Single center of being; Center of Soul; Source from which passions spring; Seat of conscience; Here we meet God.

Love
God
Neighbor
Self

Sense (Appetites)
Sight, Smell, Hearing, Touch, Taste

Passions:◄——Internal & External Powers
Morally neutral. Actually good because they motivate us. Motor to get us going; enable us to do things (11). Oriented towards Happiness; Perfected by Hope.
Concupiscible passions – Get us moving:
Pleasure (Delight)-response to possession of desired, beloved object
Pain (Sorrow)-response to union with hated object or lack of union with beloved object
Desire-seeking union with beloved object
Aversion-avoiding union with hated object
Love- our response to the beloved object as good in itself.
Hate-our response to something perceived as evil, as lacking goodness
Irascible passions – Kick in when we meet an obstacle –
   Move us towards good or getting away from evil.
Anger-tendency away from the evil of an injustice and toward the good of rectifying that injustice
Daring-tendency toward a difficult evil with the goal of conquering it
Fear-tendency away from a difficult evil
Hope–movement toward a good that we perceive will be difficult to achieve
Despair-movement away from a good as too difficult to achieve

Freedom: is the power rooted in reason and will to act or not to act. It is striving for **the good** which reason uncovers with help from the community and tradition. By free will one shapes one's life. God willed that man should be left in the hand of his own

31

Theological Virtues infused at the Sacrament of Baptism:
Faith, Hope & Charity (Love).
Moral Virtues grow through 1) education, 2) deliberate acts,
3) perseverance & struggle, purified & elevated by divine grace:
Prudence, Justice, Fortitude & Temperance

Theological Virtues: Adapt man's faculties for participation in the divine nature; They dispose Christians to live in a relationship with the Holy Trinity; The foundation of moral activity; They inform & give life to all the moral virtues. Infused by God into the soul at Baptism (CCC1812-1845).

FAITH virtue by which we believe in God & believe all that He has said & revealed to us, & that Holy Church proposes for our belief, because He is truth itself. By faith "man freely commits his entire self to God" (DV 5). For this reason, the believer seeks to know and do God's will. Living faith work(s) through charity.

HOPE virtue by which we desire the kingdom of heaven & eternal life as our happiness, placing our trust in Christ's promises and relying not on our own strength, but on the help of the grace of the Holy Spirit. It affords us joy even under trial: "Rejoice in your hope, be patient in tribulation" (1Tim2:4).

CHARITY (Love): virtue by which we love God above all things for His own sake & our neighbor as ourselves for the love of God. Jesus asks us to love as He does, *even our enemies.* Charity is the source and goal of the Christian practice. The fruits of charity are joy, peace & mercy. Charity demands beneficence & fraternal correction; it is benevolence; it fosters reciprocity & remains disinterested & generous; it is friendship & communion. It is the source & goal of the Christian practice of the virtues

Moral Virtues: firm attitudes, stable dispositions, habitual perfections of intellect & will that govern our actions, order our passions; & guide our conduct according to reason & faith. They make possible ease, self-mastery & joy leading a morally good life. The virtuous man is he who freely practices the good. Moral virtues are acquired by human effort. They are the fruit & seed of morally good acts; they dispose all the powers of the human being for communion with divine love. Perfect soul's appetites & passions.

Prudence – Disposes practical reason (conscience) to discern our true good in every circumstance & to choose the right means of achieving. "Right reason in action" (Aquinas & Aristotle). It guides the other virtues by setting rule & measure. It is prudence that immediately guides the judgment of conscience. Virtues helps us apply moral principles to a particular case without error and overcome doubts about the good to achieve and the evil to avoid. Perfect intellect.

Justice – Consists in the constant & firm will to give due to God & neighbor. Justice towards God is called the "virtue of religion." Justice towards men disposes one to respect the rights of each and to establish in human relationships the harmony that promotes equity with regard to persons and to the common good. Just man exhibits habitual right thinking & upright conduct towards neighbor. Perfects rationale appetite or will.

Fortitude – Ensures firmness in difficulties & constancy in the pursuit of the good. It strengthens the resolve to resist temptations & to overcome obstacles in the moral life. Enables one to conquer fear, even fear of death, and to face trials & persecutions. Disposes one to renounce & sacrifice life in defense of a just cause. Moderates the lower sensuous appetites.

Temperance – Moderates the attraction of pleasures & provides balance in the use of created goods. Ensures the will's mastery over instincts & keeps desires within the limits of what is honorable. The temperate person directs the sensitive appetites toward what is good & maintains a healthy discretion. Restrains impulses of concupiscence for sensible pleasures (abstinence, sobriety, chastity, continence, humility, meekness, modesty/decorum, good cheer). (CCC1803-1811)

10 Commandments

I. I am the Lord thy God. Thou shalt not have strange gods before me.
II. Thou shalt not take the name of the Lord thy God in vain
III. Remember to keep holy the Lord's day
IV. Honor thy father and they mother
V. Thou shalt not kill
VI. Thou shalt not commit adultery
VII. Thou shalt not steal
VIII. Thou shalt not bear false witness against thy neighbor.
IX. Thou shalt not covet thy neighbor's wife
X. Thou shalt not covet thy neighbor's goods.

Behavior sinks below what it means to be human if a person fails to exhibit I-X

Beatitudes

Continence of Jesus to which all Christians are called.

1. Blessed are the poor in spirit, for theirs is the kingdom of heaven
2. Blessed are the meek, for they shall possess the land.
3. Blessed are those who mourn, for they shall be comforted
4. Blessed are those who hunger and thirst for justice, for they shall be satisfied
5. Blessed are the merciful, for they shall obtain mercy
6. Blessed are the pure of heart, for they shall see God.
7. Blessed are the peacemakers for they shall be called the children of God.
8. Blessed are those who suffer persecution for justice's sake, for there is the kingdom of heaven   (Matthew 5:3-10).

Gifts of the Holy Spirit: Given to us by the Holy Spirit in order to help others. Each gift perfects the use of our faculties & powers so that we are amenable to the prompting of the Holy Spirit:

Wisdom: *Perfects our* theoretical use of the intellect, judgments about truth by giving rectitude of judgment/correct judgment about divine things.. *Happy (or Blessed) are* the Peacemakers; *they shall* be called Children of God.

Understanding: ...theoretical reasoning by grasping the 1st principle of what is said. Grasp a premise. Happy are the Pure of Heart for they shall see God.

Council: ...practical reasoning by knowing how to perform a particular action. Knowing what is the right thing to do in a particular situation (able to advise others; called prudence in self). Happy are the Merciful --- have Mercy shown them.

Fortitude: ...appetites with respect to danger threatening oneself. Ability to say "No". Hunger & Thirst for Justice-Satisfied

Knowledge: ...Know God, of books, of science. Learn! So as to help another person. ...those who Mourn-Comforted.

Piety: ...appetite with filial affection towards God. Gentle/Meek-Inherit the land.

Fear of the Lord: ...appetite in regards to tendency towards inordinate pleasure. ...Poor in Spirit – Kingdom of Heaven

Fruits of the Holy Spirit:
Perfections the Holy Spirit forms in us as the 1st fruits of eternal glory: Joy, peace, patience, kindness, goodness, generosity, gentleness, faithfulness, honesty, self-control, chastity

The Gifts of the Holy Spirit
Are habitual permanent dispositions (habitus) specifically distinct from the virtues. The gifts are necessary to salvation. The gifts are connected with Charity & grow with it. (Set down as being in us by divine inspiration.) The gifts are infused by God and by them man is disposed to become amenable to divine inspiration.
Active Life: St. Augustine distinguishes a double period of purifying preparation for wisdom. A remote preparation by active practice of the moral virtues corresponding to the gifts.
Contemplative Life: An immediate preparation, in which the soul is purified as a result of a more enlightened faith by the gift of understanding, of a firmer hope sustained by the gift of fortitude & of a more ardent charity.

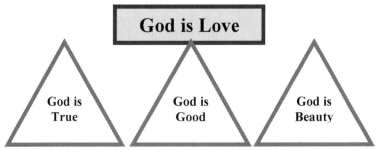

God is Love

God is True

God is Good

God is Beauty

The body is good & honorable since God has created it & will raise it on the last days.

Charity is patient & kind, it is not jealous or boastful; it is not arrogant or rude. It does not insist on its own way; it is not irritable or resentful; it does not rejoice at wrong, but rejoices in the right. It bears all things, believes all things, hopes all things, endures all things. 1Cor13:4-7

Spiritual Works of Mercy:	**Corporal Works of Mercy:**
Instruct the ignorant	Feed the hungry,
Counsel the doubtful	Give drink to the thirsty
Admonish the sinner	Give shelter to strangers
Comfort the sorrowful	Clothe the naked
Forgive injuries	Visit the sick
Bear wrongs patiently	Minister to prisoners
Pray for the living and dead	Bury the dead

Intellect - Our intellect cannot know our supernatural end without the infused light of faith. Intellect is common to men and angels.
Will - Our will cannot tend towards our supernatural end (God) unless its powers are augmented, increased more than 10x & raised to a higher order. For this the will needs a supernatural love (Charity) & a new impulse (Hope)

Seven deadly or capital sins:
Pride (Vanity) is excessive belief in one's own abilities that interferes with the individual's recognition of the grace of God. It has been called the sin from which all others arise. "Taking credit to ourselves for what was given us by God" (Baltimore Catechism-BC).
Envy is the desire for others' traits, status, abilities, or situation. "Sadness at another's welfare" (BC).
Gluttony is an inordinate desire to consume more than that which one requires. "Eating or drinking too much" (BC).
Lust is an inordinate craving for the pleasures of the body. "Strong desire for impure thoughts, words or actions" (BC).
Anger (Wrath) is manifested in the individual who spurns love and opts instead for fury.
Greed (Covetousness or Avarice) is the desire for material wealth or gain, ignoring the realm of the spiritual. "Too great a desire for money or goods." **Sloth (Acedia)** is the avoidance of physical or spiritual work. "Laziness which keeps us from doing our duty" (BC).

Compiled by Diana L. Ruzicka from information from ENDOW: Christian Anthropology, Aquinas & other studies (www.endowgroups.org), Catechism of the Catholic Church (CCC) & Catholic Distance University MA in Theology program classes (www.cdu.edu).

with his neighbor and with himself. His intellect was darkened and his will was weakened. No longer did his intellect perfectly inform his will and perfectly govern his passions and appetites. He was now prone to the three-fold concupiscence: lust of the flesh (self-indulgence), lust of the eyes (self-exaltation) and pride of life (self-worship). Instead of being in harmony with self, each other and God, all facets of life were in disharmony. Through this disordering of human nature, sin, suffering and death entered the world (Rom 5:19; Gen 3:17-19; 1 Cor 15:22). But there was hope. God promised a redeemer (Gen 3:15). See Table 2 for a brief overview of the fall and redemption as explained by Fr. Edward Leen in, *Why the Cross?* [19] We are all Adam's children by physical birth and thereby subject to the effects of the fall.[20] Through the fall of our first parents, suffering entered the world. Next we will discuss the suffering experienced by Christ that redeemed mankind and offers the possibility of our suffering having redemptive value.

Table 2 - Brief Overview of the Fall & Redemption

God, out of love through a free gift and wish to communicate Himself, created man. Man is created to know, love and serve God here on earth and to see and enjoy Him hereafter in heaven. (CCC1721). "To know God is not merely to grow in knowledge of His attributes; it is to become intimate with Him, to become conversant with His ways, and to enter into His views. To know Him is to have such an understanding of Him as will issue in interest in, and love of Him." (p99). God breathed life into man enabling him not only to live to the full aptitude of man's natural powers but he would have them taste the beatitude that He Himself enjoyed (p104). By the act of this re-creative breath, there penetrated into the substance of the soul divine grace and into the **faculties of will and intellect** the infused divine virtues of faith, hope and charity. Man's **rational powers** were further strengthened by the infused supernatural moral virtues of prudence and justice. Man's **sensitive nature** was rectified by the infused moral virtues of temperance and fortitude. The soul, by divine grace, was fashioned in **likeness of God** (p104).
Supernatural: Man is bound together by ties of supernature (sanctifying grace). As in their veins was to flow the common blood of the human family, so through their souls was to course the common life-giving stream of grace. Not only were they unified on the plane of nature, they were meant to be unified in the supernatural plane, one family & one mystical body all sharing in the same supernatural life.
Preternatural gifts: These gifts are called preternatural because they bestow something that does not belong strictly to the constitution of human nature. All this preternatural splendor of moral and intellectual beauty was bestowed on man in order that no obstacle might be presented to the progressive divinization of his soul. These gifts made him an apt receptacle for the inflow of the divine life. Man could not be tempted to what was base. But he could be tempted to aspire to what was above him.
Integrity-fortified man against the danger of conflict between sensibility and reason. By this gift, man could, without toil or effort, impose the law of reason on his sense tendencies. His passions and appetites were rightly ordered by the intellect & will. Sense was subject to reason, and reason in its turn, subjected itself readily to God. (p120). Undisturbed by passions, the will of man readily conformed itself to the will of God.
Immortality-the antidote against the natural tendency to disintegration, which belongs to all composite things (p120-121). God enabled man not to die though He did not take away radically the natural destination to death. Man was preserved from death by the preternatural gift of immortality.
Science-Man was not only dispensed from the toilsome acquisition of the moral virtues, he was also saved from the slow and painful quest of knowledge. Through infused science, man was given an understanding of human things, surpassing in range and depth anything that the world has since known (except of course our Savior and the Blessed Virgin Mary who was preserved from original sin).

Gifts/powers that constitute human nature (With which man is created in the Image of God):

Rational soul (Intellect) - By the intellect the soul has the power of acquiring knowledge that is bounded only by the limits of the created material universe. By thought, it can master and thus, in a certain sense, possess all things, though in their ideal form only.

Free Will-By his **free will** man is empowered to decide his own actions, choose between relative good things, and determine his own destiny.

Concupiscence	Explanation[2]	Moral Virtues adapt soul to receive God's grace	Corresponding theological & cardinal virtues
Pride of Life (Self-worship)	**Spiritual - Rational** Pride-the inordinate desire to excel in excess of right reason; Desire for inordinate exaltation.	**Humility** (True exaltation) Obedience; Die to self	**Faith, Hope & Charity** **Prudence** enables a person to decide early, properly & correctly.
Lust of the Eyes (Self-exaltation)	**Spiritual - Rational** Inordinate desire for things that are delectable to apprehension or imagination or some similar mode of perception (money, apparel, lust, observing a neighbor's faults for the intention of looking down on them)	**Poverty** (real wealth)	Purified by the virtue of "**Justice**" which does not seek aggrandizement at the expense of neighbor, property of reputation.
Lust of the Flesh (Self-indulgence)	**Fleshly Senses – Natural** Inordinate desire for things that sustain the nature of the body; preservation of the individual or the species (food, drink, sex).	**Chastity** (Pure love) Chaste love of God; Self-denial	Purified by the virtue of **Temperance**-against the appeals of inordinate pleasures **Fortitude**-strong against fear of pain – p128

The Fall: Each person retained the power to prefer himself to God, the power of freely choosing his final end (p121). Satan's temptation was essentially, **"This excellence, this rich life, this happiness you hold of God, you could have them in yourselves, as inherent to and as being the prerogatives of your own nature."** Like Lucifer, Adam and Eve chose, through the sin of pride, an independence from God that is intrinsically incompatible with creaturehood (p126). Through this original sin man's nature was wounded. The intellect was darkened and the will was weakened. The intellect and will would no longer function in harmony and control the passions and appetites. Man lost the preternatural gifts of integrity and science. The relationship between man and woman was ruptured as was their relationship with God. Now the moral virtues of temperance, fortitude, justice and prudence, according to the ordinary law of things, could be acquired only after years of sustained and unremitting effort. (p120). In His love for man, God removed the gift of immortality until He would send a redeemer promised in Genesis 3:15. The loss of the preternatural gifts was followed by the appearance in the soul of the three concupiscence (p143). Concupiscence are the fatal tendencies to find happiness outside of God; a perverse inclination to assert independence from God & to gratify sense & imagination in defiance of reason.

Redemption won back for the human race the power to tend toward God through grace and the exercise of the divine virtues of faith, hope and charity infused at baptism. The sacrament of baptism restored grace but not integrity. Each person is restored in Christ by being incorporated into Him mystically, the mystical body with Christ as the head. Life is a process of purification of our fallen nature. We may choose to cooperate with God's grace through daily acts of our will. In the redemption, the person is 1st restored and through the person, the nature is restored. Integrity can never be regained. But something like its equivalent must be fought for by a sustained and uncompromising resistance to the pressure of the three concupiscence. The Savior, by the sacrifice of the Passion, won the right to incorporate every human person with Himself, making each person participate in that life which dwells in the Sacred Humanity in its fullness (p151). Life is a process of purification of our fallen nature.

"You cannot be happy unless order be restored in your nature and the internal conflict in it ceases. This order cannot be established unless the disease of self-love is expelled from the soul. **Suffering in union with the sufferings of Christ most potent remedy of this disease. Suffering, by a strange paradox being made the instrument of purification, is made the means to happiness**. Accepted bravely in a Christian spirit, it removes the obstacles to the inflow of the divine life of grace. Even if, with the growth in holiness, there goes an increase in suffering, there is given additional strength to bear it and an increasing appreciation of its spiritual value. The intimacy with God that results from progress in divine grace is more than ample compensation, even in this life, for the pain that has to be borne. "*My yoke is easy and My burden light*" (Mt 11:29-30).

"*...be perfect, as your heavenly Father is perfect" (Mt 5:48)*. "Jesus didn't mean to try. He really meant it. We inherited a wounded nature (through original sin). Through the sacrament of baptism that nature is healed and elevated and so if we participate & and cooperate in the sacramental & grace-filled life, we really can be what God has called us to be, what God has created us to be. It's not a try to be your best, it's be perfect. How do we become a saint? Will it. Cooperate with God's grace."[1]

Source: Chart content from Leen, Edward. *Why the Cross?; Footnote – Quote from Fr. Tyson Wood Interview on the Journey Home.* [1]; STI-II: 77; Q84 A(2); 167 Q167, O(3)[2]

IV

And yet ours were the sufferings he bore, ours the sorrows he
carried. But we, we thought of his as someone punished,
struck by God, and brought low.
Yet he was pierced through for our faults, crushed for our sins.
On him lies a punishment that brings peace,
and through his wounds we are healed. Isaiah 53:4-5 (CTS)

Jesus Christ and Suffering

Jesus experienced three levels of suffering: physical, psychological and theological. The flogging, crowing with thorns, carrying the cross thru Jerusalem, being nailed to the cross, thirst and subsequent death by crucifixion caused excruciating physical pain. In addition to this physical pain, Jesus' mental anguish, or psychological suffering, was also very intense. Jesus endured rejection by His own people, three hours of agony, betrayal by the kiss of one of his close followers, arrest, desertion by His apostles, humiliation, accusations of false witnesses, having his face spat upon, the cowardice of Pilate, the derision of Herod, treatment with contempt as a prisoner, unjust sentencing, mocking and denial by Peter. This psychological suffering must have been immense especially since He was innocent and just.

The third type of suffering was a unique form of suffering that only the God-man could experience, theological suffering. Theological suffering is a separation from God the Father, an experience of hell. In His human flesh Jesus experienced a radical contradiction between His divinity and His humanity. "Together with this horrible weight, *encompassing the "entire" evil of the* turning *away from God* which is contained in sin, Christ, through the divine depth of his filial union with the Father, perceives in a humanly inexpressible way *this suffering which is the separation,* the rejection *by the Father,* the estrangement from God" (SD18).

Fr. Leen adds clarity to the effect of carrying the burdens of our sins as he describes the crushing weight of the three hour agony of Christ.

> In some mysterious manner, the Almighty allowed His Son to experience in the depths of His Being a realization of the consequences for Himself of His taking on His shoulders the responsibility for the crimes of humanity. He was made to feel what it was to be the head and representative of the sinful human race. In spite of His innocence, the sins of the members were laid upon Him, the head. The vast sea of human iniquity rising before Him from the past, from the present, from the future, and from the Passion itself accumulated into one vast tidal wave of black defilement and broke over His defenseless head.[21]

Jesus bore the sins of the world for our salvation and redemption. He took upon himself and bore in His flesh the sins of the whole world past, present and future. He experienced excruciating physical pain, mental anguish (psychological suffering) and separation from the Father (theological suffering).

Jesus was totally obedient to the will of the Father. United to the Father in love with the love with which He loved the world, Jesus suffered His passion (SD 17). Christ suffered voluntarily and innocently (SD 18). Isaiah describes the suffering servant which, in the light of the New Testament, we identify as Jesus Christ and His redemptive suffering (Table 3).

Table 3. Christ's Redemptive Suffering
"He had no form or comeliness that we should look at Him, and no beauty that we should desire Him. He was despised and rejected by men; *a man of sorrows,* and acquainted with grief; and as one from whom men hide their faces. He was despised, and we esteemed him not. Surely He has borne our griefs and carried our sorrows; yet we esteemed Him stricken, smitten by God, and afflicted. But He was wounded for our transgressions, He was bruised for our iniquities; upon Him was the chastisement that made us whole, and with His stripes we are healed. All we like sheep have gone astray we have turned everyone to his own way; and *the Lord has laid on him the iniquity of us all".* Isaiah 53:2-6
Source: The Holy Bible, Revised Standard Version, Catholic Edition

The crucifixion is the revelation of God's absolute love.[22] For a person to sacrifice their life for a righteous man is one thing. But Christ gave His life for all sinners. "No passion moves us more readily and more deeply than love. And when love is gratuitous, wholly disinterested, when we have insulted Him who loves us, and, instead of condemning us forever, He suffers and dies for us, words cannot express our wonderment."[23]

V

I have been crucified with Christ;
it is no longer I who live, but Christ who lives in me;
and the life I now live in the flesh I live by faith in the Son of God,
who loved me and gave himself for me. St. Paul (Gal 2:20)

Effects of Christ's Redemption

In redeeming mankind, Jesus enabled man to be restored to grace with God. This is initiated through the sacrament of baptism. Jesus commissioned the apostles to teach, make disciples and baptize (Mt 28:19-20). Through this baptism man becomes part of the Church which is the mystical body of Christ with Christ as the head. Life as part of the Mystical Body of Christ is a new type of life.

> A Christian no longer lives his life --- or is at least no longer meant to live his life --- in isolation. By baptism he is incorporated into Christ, made a member of Christ's Mystical Body. But this is "membership" unlike any other. One who is a member of the Mystical Body is united with Christ, shares Christ's life, participates in Christ's human acts and merit; through the Eucharist Jesus lives in him, and he in Jesus. The union between Christ and the member is not merely moral, a bond between leader and followers; it is, as one writer expresses it, "real" and "ontological." These words signify a union, a sharing of life, which exceeds every other relationship in our experience to the point that a member of Christ can speak of Christ as his very identity.[24]

"The redemption won back for the human race the power to tend towards God through grace and the exercise of the divine virtues of faith, hope and charity."[25] "Christ proposes a life lived in a new dimension, a life of grace and faith."[26] However, man still lacks integrity, the right ordering of his soul. Man struggles against self-exaltation, self-indulgence and self-worship (concupiscence). "In the redemption, it is the person that is first restored, and through the person, the nature."[27] Therefore, this life involves a process of purification. Each decision we make, each choice that is put before us daily is an opportunity to choose for or against God. Will we be disciples of Christ? Will we pick up our cross? Will we say no to self-exultation, self-indulgence and self-worship? This "saying no to self," whether in the physical or spiritual realm causes suffering. Dr. Peter Kreeft points out how modern man has convoluted the whole purpose and meaning of life. "The most important thing in life is reconciliation with God, union with God and conformity to God. However modern man has made the most important thing in life conquering suffering and attaining pleasure, comfort and power by man's conquest of nature. Thus modern man does not understand the meaning of suffering or of pleasure."[28]

Dom van Zeller summarized the effect of our redemption in relation to suffering.

> In itself, suffering is an evil: it is a negation of a
> particular good. Happiness, on the other hand, is

> something positive: it is a good toward which we
> have a right-ordered appetite. But once given the
> Passion, suffering becomes a good. A new element
> has entered in, turning the negation into an
> affirmation: suffering becomes a positive statement,
> proclaiming service, praise, union and love... The
> cross is an expression of discipleship.[29]

Suffering, in itself, is not a good. However, Christ has transformed suffering. Christ changed human suffering through his passion by linking it with love (SD 18). He suffers with us and has now shown us how to suffer. Jesus calls Christian "to bear up" and carry the cross daily (Mt 10:38, Lk 9:23). "If anyone wants to be followers of mine, let him renounce himself and take up his cross and follow me. Anyone who wants to save his life will lose it; but anyone who loses his life for My sake and for the sake of the Gospel will save it" (Mk 8:34-38). Jesus conquered sin by His obedience in love unto death and He overcame death by His resurrection (SD14). "To transform the cross from being an instrument of torture into an instrument of salvation, man must bravely accept life as a cross to be borne daily."[30] "Suffering amid the brokenness of the world is not something merely to be endured with courage, but to be redeemed by love."[31]

Dr. Peter Kreeft summarizes three things that Jesus did to solve the problem of suffering:

> First, he came. He suffered with us. He wept.
> **Second, in becoming man He transformed the**

meaning of our suffering; it is now part of His work of redemption. Our death pangs become birth pangs for heaven, not only for ourselves but also for those we love. Third, He died and rose. Dying, He paid the price for sin and opened heaven to us; rising, He transformed death from a hole into a door, from an end into a beginning (bold mine).[32]

Now we return to Betty's story.

VI

Rejoice, beloved, in the measure that you share Christ's
sufferings. When his glory is revealed, you will rejoice exultantly.
Happy are you when you are insulted for the sake of Christ, for
then God's Spirit in its glory has come to rest on you.
1 Peter 4:13-14

Betty's Suffering – Part 2

At one point during her illness Darrel and Betty were
lying in their marital bed which had been moved to the
downstairs dining room. The nurse friend was silently praying at
the bedside the four mysteries of the rosary and the divine mercy
chaplet. At one point Darrel began to sob. He cried with great
anguish and arose from the bed clutching his chest experiencing
excruciating chest pain. He later related that he had had a
spiritual experience with his wife. He described that they were
walking together and were greeted by relatives who had
previously died. He saw the glow of an orange light and he knew
Betty would be alright. Suddenly Betty dropped his hand and he
awoke. It was not his time to go. The pain Darrel was
experiencing was an intense anguish anticipating the loss of his
wife of forty years.[33]

Betty refused opioid analgesics during her illness stating she was
not in pain and did not want them. Why? Was she uniting her
sufferings with those of Christ so as to participate in His
redemption? Redemptive suffering does not preclude the use of

opioids or other medications for the appropriate management of pain. In fact the appropriate pain medication and the relief it provides can be a great blessing for those suffering from physical pain.

Betty had only recently begun to study the Bible and develop a knowledge of Jesus Christ through a non-denominational Bible study. Could God have been educating her through the suffering? She had not yet been baptized and did not have an intellectual knowledge of the concept of redemptive suffering. Could someone's suffering be redemptive without their awareness or will? Was she lingering until she knew Darrel had accepted Christ? Was she lingering to ensure Darrel was taken care of? The story of Darrel and Betty will unfold throughout this paper as we explore the meaning of redemptive suffering.

In addition to an introduction to the suffering encountered by Betty and Darrel Kaiser, the preceding has introduced the concept of suffering, differentiated it from evil and pain, and briefly discussed the nature of man, effects of the fall and Christ's redemptive suffering to which human suffering is to be linked to be redemptive. The next section will explore suffering as described in the New Testament and then focus specifically on the words of St. Paul to the Colossians.

VII

Then Jesus told his disciples,
"If any man would come after Me,
let him deny himself and take up his cross and follow me.
For whoever would save his life will lose it,
and whoever loses his life for My sake will find it. Mt 16:24-25

The New Testament and Redemptive Suffering

In an analysis of the concept of suffering in the New Testament, three themes emerged: (1) Christians will suffer. (2) Suffering can be offered for oneself and others and (3) there are examples of how to respond to suffering.

Christians Will Suffer

All Christians will suffer. Being a Christian does not ensure a life without struggle or suffering. "Indeed all who desire to live a godly life in Christ Jesus will be persecuted" (2 Tim 3:10-17). To be a Christian requires that we pick up our cross and follow Christ daily. St. Paul instructs the Philippians that they are to suffer with Christ as he himself is doing, "For it has been granted to you that for the sake of Christ you should not only believe in him but also suffer for His sake engaging in the same conflict which you saw and now hear to be mine" (Phil 1:29).

Paul instructs the Christians in Rome to suffer with Christ. "We are children of God whom we can call "Abba! Father!... And if children, then heirs, heirs of God and fellow heirs with Christ, provided we suffer with Him in order that we may also be glorified with Him" (Rom 8:15, 17).

Suffering for Self and Others

All Christians will experience suffering. It is what we do with that suffering which makes it redemptive. Suffering can be offered for the good of others (1 Tm 1:15-16; 2 Tm 2:8-13; Eph 3:13; 2 Cor 1:5-7) or to redeem oneself (Jas 1:12; Lk 22:28-30, Phil 3:8-11). In regards to suffering for others, St. Paul saw himself as the foremost sinner (1 Tm 1:15). He had severely persecuted the Christians prior to his conversion on the road to Damascus. Through all the suffering he endured in preaching the gospel, he remained faithful and an example of Christ's mercy. "The suffering and humiliation Paul endured was redemptive for it freed sinners of fear and made them look to God for mercy."[34] In the second example, Paul specifically instructs the bishop Timothy that he endured suffering so that the elect may obtain salvation, "Therefore I endured everything for the sake of the elect, that they also may obtain the salvation which in Christ Jesus goes with eternal glory" (2 Tm 2:10). Thirdly he explains to the Ephesians that his suffering is for their glory (Eph 3:13). In the fourth example St. Paul describes the importance of his and his companions' suffering and calls the Corinthians to share in that suffering:

> For we share abundantly in Christ's sufferings, so through Christ we share abundantly in comfort

> too. If we are afflicted, it is for your comfort and
> salvation; and if we are comforted, it is for your
> comfort, which you experience when you patiently
> endure the same sufferings that we suffer. Our
> hope for you is unshaken; for we know that as you
> share in our sufferings, you will also share in our
> comfort (2 Cor 1:5-7).

The preceding are four examples of suffering for the redemption of others. Next are three examples of suffering for the redemption of one's own soul. "Suffering is redemptive if it makes you humbler and brings you closer to God."[35] After Jesus admonished His apostles for disputing over whom amongst them is the greatest, He instructed them to serve. Serving is a suffering caused by dying to oneself for the other. Jesus then elaborated that those who endured trials with Him will have a place in His kingdom and the apostles will sit on the thrones judging the twelve tribes of Israel (Lk 22:28-30). Next St. James declares blessed the man who endures trials, for when he has stood the test he will receive the crown of life which God has promised to those who love Him (Jas 1:12). In the last example St. Paul describes his own suffering and hope of attaining redemption:

> Indeed I count everything as loss because of the
> surpassing worth of knowing Christ Jesus my
> Lord. For His sake I have suffered loss of all
> things and count them as refuse, in order that I
> may gain Christ and be found in Him not having a
> righteousness of my own, based on law, but that
> which is through faith in Christ, the righteousness
> from God that depends on faith; that I may know

> him and the power of His resurrection, and may
> share His sufferings, becoming like Him in His
> death, that if possible I may attain the resurrection
> from the dead (Phil 3:8-11).

Paul desires to share in Christ's sufferings to attain the resurrection from the dead and to bring others to Christ. As Christians we can all expect to suffer as Christ. We can suffer to redeem ourselves and others. How then does the New Testament describe that we respond as we encounter suffering?

How to Respond to Suffering

The classic description of redemptive suffering is described by St. Paul, "Now I rejoice in my sufferings for your sake, and in my flesh I complete what is lacking in Christ's afflictions for the sake of His body, that is the Church (Col 1:24)." In the next section w will explore Bible commentaries, Church documents and writings of Church leaders explaining the meaning of each section of this verse. Here let us specifically address the attitude and behavior one should demonstrate toward suffering in general. St. Paul rejoices or is happy to suffer for Christ's sake. He is not happy just to suffer without meaning. He rejoices because he suffers for Christ's sake. So rejoicing, joy or happiness is a key approach or perhaps an outcome of Christian suffering (Mt 5:11-12; Acts 5:41; 1 Pt 4:13). St. Peter instructs the Church to follow the example of Christ and be submissive to masters in all respect. Individuals are to be kind and gentle even if their masters are overbearing. They should endure pain while

suffering unjustly and take it patiently. If they are reviled, like
Christ, they should not revile in turn. If they suffer they should
not threaten. They are to trust and let God, who judges justly,
judge. They are to die to sin and live righteously (1 Pt 2:19-25).
To the Philippians St. Paul instructs Christians to, "Do all things
without grumbling or questioning that you may be blameless and
innocent, children of God without blemish in the midst of a
crooked and perverse generation, among whom you shine as light
in the world, holding fast the word of life" (Phil 2:14-16). In
several verses St. Paul describes how he faced trials and
tribulations and recommended others do so. Approach your own
suffering with unshaken hope. Don't let your own or the
sufferings of others dishearten or discourage you or cause you to
lose confidence (2 Cor 1:5-7; Eph 3:13; Heb 10:32). Respond to
affliction, hardships, calamities, beatings, imprisonments,
tumults, labors, hunger, watching and waiting by exhibiting
purity, knowledge, forbearance, kindness, the Holy Spirit,
genuine love, truthful speech, the power of God and with the
weapon of righteousness. These attributes are to be exhibited in
situation when the person is honored or dishonored, in ill repute
and in good repute. When speaking to the elders from Ephesus
St. Paul instructed them to endure trials with humility, though
shedding tears are also acceptable. (Acts 20:18-37). St. Paul
recommends that Christians have compassion on prisoners and
joyfully accept the plundering of their property. He again

reiterates the importance of endurance so that they may do the will of God and receive what is promised (Heb 10:32). To the Romans St. Paul instructs, "Rejoice in your hope, be patient in tribulation, be constant in prayer" (Rom 12:12) and later, "Bless those who persecute you; bless and do not curse them" (Rom 12:14), "Repay no one evil for evil, but take thought for what is noble in the sight of all. If possible, so far as it depends upon you, live peaceably with all. Beloved, never avenge yourselves, but leave it to the wrath of God; for it is written, 'Vengeance is mine, I will repay, says the Lord.' No, 'if your enemy is hungry, feed him; if he is thirsty, give him drink; for by so doing you will heap burning coals upon his head." Do not be overcome by evil, but overcome evil with good" (Rom 12:17-21). St. James also instructs believers to endure trials (Jas 1:12).

Saints Peter, Paul, James, John, Matthew and Luke, in giving examples of Jesus' behavior, all describe how to approach suffering. St. Paul guides us to offer it for others, for the body for Christ, for the Church. In suffering our disposition must be one of receptivity and openness to grace. Redemptive suffering calls forth the virtue of perseverance (SD 23), courage and fortitude (SD 25) in bearing our sufferings. To cooperate in Christ's redemptive suffering, we are to bear our suffering with resignation and love and, by an act of the will, suffer for sinners and others.[36]

Before we continue with St. Paul's *Letter to the Colossians*, let us return to Betty's story.

VIII

Greater love has no man than this,
that a man lay down his life for his friends.
You are my friends if you do what I command you. (Jn 15:13-14)

Betty's Suffering – Part 3

Betty refused opioid analgesics during her illness initially verbally, later by spitting the medication out of her mouth and refusing to swallow. Two friends, who were nurses, attempted to medicate Betty as she moaned in bed the nights they were watching her so that Darrel could sleep. Later Darrel shared that Betty always moaned in her sleep (an important fact to share with a nurse watching her). As Betty's health deteriorated, Darrel became exhausted from caring for her each day. He was found sobbing breathlessly at the kitchen sink when the hospice staff arrived. Later the hospice nurse offered to give Betty a morphine suppository. One of the nurse friends yelled from the room where Betty was lying, "She doesn't want any." When Betty was not dead a week later, the hospice nurse again approached Darrel to administer a morphine suppository. Betty's condition was indeed dire. She had no peripheral pulses, her eyes rolled in the sockets --- it took too much energy to focus them. She was not speaking. Her breathing was labored and she was oozing fluids requiring frequent bed changes and protectant applied to her rectal area to prevent bedsores. Why was she still alive? This time it was Darrel who responded to the hospice nurse's second offer of a morphine suppository, "I know what you are trying to do. She doesn't want the morphine." However, that night he came to one of the nurse friends and said, "If Betty does not die tomorrow, I will need to give her that morphine." In response, the nurses explained, "Darrel, I do not know what is keeping Betty alive. For all intents and purposes, she should be dead. But she is holding on for some reason. If you give the morphine, you will kill her and that will hurt your soul because you will know why you are doing it. When we have children we take care of our children. We have to totally take care of them for many years. That is what love is about. It is about getting out of yourself and helping another person. What you are doing now, is real love. Not many husbands would do this. Darrel, I do not know why Betty is still alive but if I would have to guess, she is waiting for your sister to return. Kathy will be here on Saturday." It would be Saturday in two days.

Was Betty's suffering redemptive? Was she uniting her suffering with that of Christ in His passion? Unfortunately she was not able to communicate so this is unknown. Was Darrel's suffering redemptive? He certainly was not uniting his suffering with Christ's in a conscious act of the will. He was in agony over the loss of his wife. Why would God take the bride of his childhood? Why would God take the woman to whom he had been married 40 years? Darrel had been baptized at a Lutheran church but hadn't attended service throughout his adult life. His wife and career had been his God. Could his suffering be redemptive without intentionally uniting it with Christ's?

Now, we return to the New Testament specifically exploring several commentaries on what St. Paul said to the Colossians around 62A.D.

IX

"Now I rejoice in my sufferings for your sake, and in my flesh
I complete what is lack in Christ's afflictions
for the sake of his body, that is the Church." Col 1:24

New Testament - Colossians 1:24

In St. Paul's epistle to the Colossians quoted above St. Paul (1) rejoices in suffering. (2) He suffers immensely for proclaiming the gospel. (3) He completes what is lacking in Christ's suffering. (4) And he suffers for others, the Church. These concepts will be explored.

Rejoicing in Suffering

First, St. Paul rejoices in suffering for his brethren. This joy is actually the result of a profound interior conversion. When an individual suffers they seek to know why. Through this interior struggle the meaning is revealed and ultimately joy can become the result as explained by Pope St. John Paul II:

> Christ does not explain in the abstract the reasons
> for suffering, but before all else He says: "Follow
> me!" Come! Take part through your suffering in
> this work of saving the world, a salvation achieved
> through my suffering! Through my Cross.
> Gradually, *as the individual takes up his cross,*
> spiritually uniting himself to the Cross of Christ,
> the salvific meaning of suffering is revealed
> before him. He does not discover this meaning at
> his own human level, but at the level of the
> suffering of Christ. At the same time, however,
> from this level of Christ the salvific meaning of
> suffering *descends to man's level* and becomes, in

a sense, the individual's personal response. It is
then that man finds in his suffering interior peace
and even spiritual joy (SD 26).

Joy in the midst of suffering is described by Jesus at the
conclusion of the beatitudes in the Sermon on the Mount,
"Blessed are you when men revile you and persecute you and
utter all kinds of evil against you falsely on my account. Rejoice
and be glad, for your reward is great in heaven, for so men
persecuted the prophets who were before you" (Mt 5:11-12).
Jesus did not promise we would not suffer. Indeed He advised us
to expect suffering and to respond by rejoicing and hoping in our
heavenly reward. At the same time, however, Jesus spent much
of his ministry relieving the suffering of others. We are called to
do the same. As God walks with us in our suffering, we are to
walk with others in theirs.

Joy in the midst of suffering is also described by St. Luke.
After the descent of the Holy Spirit, when St. Peter and the
apostles were imprisoned, released by an angel, found again
teaching in the temple, brought before the council and the high
priest, questioned, beaten and again told not to teach, "They left
the presence of the council, rejoicing that they were counted
worthy to suffer dishonor for the name" (Acts 5:41). They also
did not stop preaching and teaching Jesus Christ (Acts 5:42). St.
Peter instructs Christians to rejoice during suffering: "But rejoice
in so far as you share Christ's sufferings, that you may also
rejoice and be glad when His glory is revealed" (1 Pet 4:13).[37]

When we unite our suffering (physical and psychological) with those of Christ, we proclaim the gospel. We proclaim our belief and hope in Jesus Christ. With this hope and confidence we can radiate joy in the midst of, perhaps, and certainly after persevering in faith through the suffering. The next section investigates the type of suffering described by Paul.

The Sufferings of St. Paul

What is this suffering which gives St. Paul cause to rejoice? We alluded to it above. The word used for St. Paul's suffering is *thlipsis*. This term is associated with the hardship of those proclaiming the gospel. It is reportedly never used in describing Jesus' passion.[38] So when St. Paul says that he "rejoices in his suffering," he is rejoicing in the hardships that he encounters when witnessing to and/or proclaiming the good news of Jesus Christ.[39] Our suffering may be nowhere near that experienced by St. Paul. And though St. Paul's sufferings were nowhere near the intensity of that suffered by Christ during His passion, the sufferings that St. Paul experienced while proclaiming the gospel were quite severe. St. Paul was imprisoned, beaten "often near death," whipped, beaten with rods, stoned, shipwrecked, adrift at sea. He was in danger from rivers, robbers, his own people, Gentiles, in the city, wilderness, at sea, and from false brethren. He suffered toil and hardship. He experienced many sleepless nights, was hungry, thirsty, cold and exposed. He also suffered from the daily pressures and anxieties for all the churches (2 Cor 11:23-29). Of note is that the five times that he was whipped at the hands of the Jews, he received forty lashes less one" (2 Cor 11:24). This must have been particularly humiliating since he, himself had been an honored Jew, a Pharisee who studied at the feet of the great Rabbi Gamaliel. Forty lashes were the number that would kill a man. In describing that he received 40 less one, St. Paul is reiterating that, with each of these five lashings, he was almost beaten to death. In Lystra, at the instigation of Jews from Antioch and Iconium, St. Paul was stoned in the city streets, thought to be dead and dragged from the city (Acts 14:18-19). Through all these sufferings St. Paul rejoices. He is an example of faith and hope for each one of us. He suffered the loss of all things but willingly did so in order that he may gain Christ (Phil 3:8). St. Paul then states that the sufferings in which he rejoices completes what is lacking in Christ's afflictions.

Complete what is lacking

What could be lacking in *Christ's afflictions*? The Church teaches that nothing is lacking in Christ's redemptive offering of Himself through His passion, death and resurrection (SD 24). He accomplished the work that His Father gave Him to do (Jn 17:4). Objectively redemption and salvation are available to each one of us. However, subjectively, we have the choice to cooperate with or partake in Christ's redemption. St. Alphonsus explains the importance of cooperating with Christ (e.g. subjective redemption) in a commentary on Col 1:24:

> Can it be that Christ's passion alone was insufficient to save us? It left nothing more to be done, it was entirely sufficient to save all men. However, for the merits of the Passion to be applied to us, according to St. Thomas (Summa theologias, 3, 49, 3), we need to cooperate (subjective redemption) by patiently bearing the trials God sends us, so as to become like our head, Christ.[40]

St. Paul also describes his own participation in the

redemptive suffering of Christ:

> But we have this treasure in earthen vessels, to show that the transcendent power belongs to God and not to us. We are afflicted in every way, but not crushed; perplexed, but not driven to despair; persecuted, but not forsaken; struck down but not destroyed; always carrying in the body the death of Jesus, **so that the life of Jesus may also be manifested in our bodies**. For while we live we are always being given up to death for Jesus' sake, **so that the life of Jesus may be manifested in our mortal flesh**. So death is at work in us, but life in you…For **it is all for your sake**, so that as grace extends to more and more people it may increase thanksgiving, to the glory of God. (2 Cor 4:7-12, 15; bold mine).

Jesus invites each of us into His redemptive suffering as

explained by Pope St. John Paul II:

The Redeemer suffered in place of man and for man. Every man has *his own share in the Redemption.* Each one is also *called to share in that suffering* through which the Redemption was accomplished. He is called to share in that suffering through which all **human suffering has also been redeemed**. In bringing about the Redemption through suffering, **Christ** *has* **also** *raised human suffering to the level of the Redemption.* Thus each man, in his suffering, can also become a sharer in the redemptive suffering of Christ. (SD19; bold mine).

Each person's suffering can build up the body of Christ, the Church. Pope St. John Paul II explanation that suffering in love builds up the body of Christ and helps to redeem the world:

The Redemption, accomplished through satisfactory love, *remains always open to all love* expressed in *human suffering.* In this dimension— the dimension of love—**the Redemption which has already been completely accomplished is, in a certain sense, constantly being accomplished**. Christ achieved the Redemption completely and to the very limits but at the same time he did not bring it to a close. In this redemptive suffering, through which the Redemption of the world was accomplished, Christ opened himself from the beginning to every human suffering and constantly does so. Thus with this openness to every human suffering, Christ has accomplished the world's Redemption through his own suffering. For, at the same time, **this Redemption, even though it was completely achieved by Christ's suffering, lives on and in its own special way develops in the history of man. It lives and develops as the**

body of Christ, the Church, and in this dimension every human suffering, by reason of the loving union with Christ, completes the suffering of Christ. (SD 24, bold mine).

When we embrace our cross, uniting it to that of Christ and offering it up to God for the redemption of souls, we have the possibility of sharing in His redemptive mission.

Suffering for Others

Christ's redemptive sacrifice was sufficient to redeem the world. However, in God's infinite wisdom and love, He allows us to participate in Christ's redemption by uniting our suffering to that of Christ to aid our brothers and sisters. Pope Saint John Paul II provides valuable insights on how Jesus transformed human suffering and it can be offered for others:

A source of joy is found in the *overcoming of the sense of the uselessness of suffering,* a feeling that is sometimes very strongly rooted in human suffering. This feeling not only consumes the person interiorly, but seems to make him a burden to others. The person feels condemned to receive help and assistance from others and at the same time seems useless to himself. The discovery of the salvific meaning of suffering in union with Christ *transforms* this depressing *feeling.* Faith in sharing in the suffering of Christ brings with it the interior certainty that **the suffering person "completes what is lacking in Christ's afflictions"; the certainty that in the spiritual dimension of the work of Redemption *he is serving*, like Christ, *the salvation of his brothers*** *and sisters.* Therefore he is carrying out an irreplaceable service. In the Body of Christ, which is ceaselessly born of the Cross of the Redeemer, it is precisely suffering permeated by the spirit of Christ's sacrifice that *is the irreplaceable mediator and author of the good things* which are indispensable for the world's salvation. It is suffering, more than anything else, which clears the way for the grace which transforms human souls. Suffering, more than anything else makes present in the history of humanity the powers of the Redemption. In that "cosmic" struggle between the spiritual powers of good and evil, spoken of in the Letter to the Ephesians (6:12), **human sufferings, united to the redemptive suffering of Christ,** *constitute a special support for the powers of good,* **and open the way to the victory of these salvific powers.**

And so the Church sees in all Christ's suffering brothers and sisters as it were a *multiple subject of his supernatural power.* How often is it precisely to them that the pastors of the Church appeal and precisely from them that they seek help and support! The Gospel of suffering is being written unceasingly, and it speaks unceasingly with the words of this strange paradox: the springs of divine power gush forth precisely in the midst of human weakness. **Those who share in the sufferings of Christ preserve in their own sufferings a very special** *particle of the* **infinite** *treasure* **of the world's Redemption, and can share this treasure with others** (SD 27; bold mine).

Jesus instructed us to suffer for others, "Greater love has no man than this, that a man lay down his life for his friends (Jn

15:15)." God choose some to participate in the salvation of souls by enduring suffering that is over and above what they need for themselves."[41] Mother Angelica explains that,

> most Christians are not asked to make the supreme sacrifice but God chose some to participate in the salvation of souls, not by giving up their lives, but by enduring suffering that are over and above what they need for themselves. All those whose suffering is redemptive can say with St. Paul, 'Never lose confidence because of the trials that I go through on your account; they are your glory' (Eph 3:13).[42]

It is Jesus who continues to suffer in the Christian for the good of all mankind. Jesus suffers with those who are suffering. Pope Benedict XVI further describes this concept:

> God cannot suffer, but he can **suffer with**. Man is worth so much to God that he himself became man in order to suffer with man in an utterly real way—in flesh and blood—as is revealed to us in the account of Jesus' Passion. Hence in all human suffering we are joined by one who experiences and carries that suffering with us; hence consolatio is present in all suffering, the consolation of God's compassionate love—and so the star of hope rises. The saints were able to make the great journey of human existence in the way that Christ had done before them, because they were brimming with great hope (SS 39).

X

*"By enduring the toil of work
in union with Christ crucified for us,
man in a way collaborates with the Son of God
for the redemption of humanity."* Pope St. John Paul II

Two Popes Describe How to Suffer Redemptively

Much of the New Testament section on how to respond to suffering addressed how to suffer redemptively. Therefore, this section will only add two explanations from our popes.

In his encyclical *Laborem Excerens* (On Human Work), Pope St. John Paul II describes that even the suffering in our everyday toil can have redemptive value: "By enduring the toil of work in union with Christ crucified for us, man in a way collaborates with the Son of God for the redemption of humanity. He shows himself a true disciple of Christ by carrying the cross in his turn every day in the activity that he is called upon to perform" (LE 27).

Pope Benedict XVI further explains how to offer up our daily sufferings:

> There used to be a form of devotion—perhaps less practiced today but quite widespread not long ago—that included the idea of "offering up" the minor daily hardships that continually strike at us like irritating "jabs", thereby giving them a meaning. Of course, there were some exaggerations and perhaps unhealthy applications of this devotion, but we need to ask ourselves

whether there may not after all have been
something essential and helpful contained within
it. What does it mean to offer something up?
Those who did so were convinced that they could
insert these little annoyances into Christ's great
"com-passion" so that they somehow became part
of the treasury of compassion so greatly needed by
the human race. In this way, even the small
inconveniences of daily life could acquire
meaning and contribute to the economy of good
and of human love. Maybe we should consider
whether it might be judicious to revive this
practice ourselves (SS 40).

It is important to note that, like in prayer where we unite
our will with the Will of the Father, in redemptive suffering our
effort should be to place our pain and suffering in Jesus'
suffering and Passion rather than to bring His suffering into
ours."[43]

XI

"Prayer takes on extraordinary power to win graces
For the one praying and for all mankind
When it is united with patient suffering."
Pope St. John Paul II

Effects of Redemptive Suffering

The effects of Redemptive Suffering are both natural and supernatural. In the natural realm, our perseverance in faith and trust in God unleashes hope:

> Perseverance unleashes hope, which maintains in him the conviction that suffering will not get the better of him, that it will not deprive him of his dignity as a human being, a dignity linked to awareness of the meaning of life. And indeed this meaning makes itself known together with *the working of God's love,* which is the supreme gift of the Holy Spirit. The more he shares in this love, man rediscovers himself more and more fully in suffering: he rediscovers the "soul" which he thought he had "lost"(Mk 8:35, Lk 9:24, Jn 12:25) because of suffering. (SD 23)

Dr. Scott Hahn and Curtis Mitch elaborate on the effect of suffering for Jesus' sake:

> Suffering brings great benefit to ourselves and others. On the one hand, it purifies us of selfishness and makes us sharers in Christ's redemptive work (Phil 3:10, 2 Cor 1:5, Col 1:24, 1 Pet1:6-7). On the other, it pushes the gospel into the world as believers bear witness to the Lord Jesus through persecution and martyrdom (1 Cor 4:9-13, 2 Cor 5:11). Scripture depicts suffering as

a privilege (Acts 5:41) and so challenges us to embrace it and not simply endure it (Rom8:17, 1Pet4:12-16).[44]

We proclaim the gospel to the world by remaining faithful throughout the suffering thus allowing the world to see our Christian's faith and hope. In redemptive suffering there is an additional supernatural effect on the Mystical Body of Christ or the Communion of the Saints when the suffering is united to Christ's cross in love.[45] "…Suffering opens the door for grace to transform us and the world in love."[46]

When our neighbor sees us bearing sufferings with courage, love and unwavering faith in Christ, we can "set our neighbors free."[47] When Christians saw St. Paul's fidelity and fortitude, it helped them overcome fear and cowardice and be brave. St. Paul's suffering and humiliation freed sinners of fear and made them look to God for mercy.[48] The examples of Christ and St. Paul living a holy Christian life through suffering released and set the people free from the bondage of sin.[49] This effect can be the consequence of witness suffering which itself gives courage or redemptive suffering which mystically transforms the Body of Christ (Col 2:2). When we unite our suffering with the sufferings of Christ for others in love, that love binds us together. That love or charity manifests the Holy Spirit, a powerful source of grace for ourselves and others. If we just observe with our senses and exteriorly reflect on the Passion, we lose a great opportunity for interior conversion. When we unite our sufferings with His for the salvation of souls, Jesus draws us to Himself, so that we might share by experience in His "lifting up" (Jn 12:32).[50] As truly part of the Mystical Body of Christ the suffering experienced by one member can serve as a conduit of grace and vicariously "do duty" for the punishment of another.[51] Fr. Dom von Zeller also describes the effect of redemptive suffering:

> The Christian who truly enters into the Passion by cooperating in the searing experience of accepted suffering acts as a viaduct along which the graces of conversion and pardon are conveyed to the sinner. Acting with Christ and as Christ acts, the Christian saint puts at the disposal of all the merit of His labor. While there can obviously be no guarantee that the sufferings of one man, however holy, will be allocated to the redemption or sanctification of any one particular nominee, it can be confidently supposed that not only do the penances of one avail for the good of all, but that the intention to help individuals by the process of vicarious expiation will be taken into account....If, when we pray for particular people, we have the assurance that they are receiving grace from God, it is only reasonable to believe that the same thing happens when we suffer for them. It is not as though they are getting grace from us: they are getting it from GOD *through* us.[52]

It is difficult to find actual examples of the supernatural effect of redemptive suffering. The following section provides some modern day examples of redemptive suffering. Towards the end, Archbishop Fulton Sheen provides a poignant example of the supernatural effect of redemptive suffering. We will then conclude Betty's life journey, the experience of the death of a father and father-in-law in which the father-in-law was rapidly over-sedated, unable to eat and died, followed by the conclusion of this paper.

XII

"It is part of the discipline of God to make His loved ones perfect through trail and suffering. Only by carrying the Cross can one reach the Resurrection."
---Venerable Archbishop Fulton Sheen

Modern Examples of Redemptive Suffering

In the writing of St. Rose of Lima (1586-1617) she shared that Jesus asked her to, "Let all men know that grace comes after tribulation. Let them know that without the burden of affliction it is impossible to reach the height of grace. Let them know that the gifts of grace increase as struggles increase. Take care not to stray and be deceived. This is the only true stairway to paradise, and without the cross they can find no road to climb to heaven."[53] Grace, the life of God within us, the power that restores us to union with God, comes to us through our faithfulness through suffering.

Mother Teresa (1910-1997) expounded on this in a speech I had the pleasure of attending in 1982 in San Francisco when she spoke on the beautiful gift of suffering: "Suffering is a gift of God. It is a sign that we have come so close to Him that we can share His passion; suffering is a gift, a gift that purifies us, that sanctifies us."[54] Mother Teresa understood how suffering has the power to unite us with the passion of Christ. It is a gift that has the capacity to purify us and help us to grow in holiness. It has the power to redeem us if we suffer in love with Christ. (See Appendix A)

A dear friend of mine experienced first-hand the suffering of a wayward daughter (Appendix B). In her anguish and fear, Jesus asked her to carry His cross. When the cross became too heavy for her to bear, He lightened her load albeit briefly.[55] Navy Admiral Jeremiah Denton shared his experience as a former prisoner of war in Vietnam and how the simple prayer, ***"Sacred Heart of Jesus, I give myself to you"*** flooded him with peace through the intense torture he suffered (Appendix C).

The Venerable Archbishop Fulton Sheen shared two very poignant stories of the value and effect of redemptive suffering. In one story he tells about a woman who was brokenhearted and distressed due to the criminal behavior of her son who was in prison. Archbishop Sheen explained that our love of neighbor is in essence to be a sin bearer. This mother carried on her shoulders the sins of her son. As he listened to this mother pour out her grief, the Holy Spirit impressed upon Archbishop Fulton Sheen's heart the words from Isaiah 53:4, 5, "she had born his griefs, carried his sorrows... and the chastisement of his peace was upon her and it would only be by her stripes that he would be healed." He revealed that the mother had no serious sins but she was carrying her son's sins due to the great love she had for him. This, Archbishop Sheen said, was the closest we can ever get on earth to the love of God, to understand what God did for us (Appendix D).

Saint Paul of the Cross (1694-1775) shared that to meditate on Jesus' passion is the sacred path by which we reach union with God. We have the option of suffering and dying, suffering and not dying or "better to do neither suffer nor die but only turn perfectly to the will of God."[56] He further explains that love is the unifying force or virtue. By uniting our sufferings in love with Christ, the lover (us) is transformed into the one loved (Jesus Christ).

In the first example St. Rose of Lima shared a revelation from God. Mother Teresa asked a women to bear her own pain and suffering as a gift from God. Betty shared her personal experience with suffering. Archbishop Sheen shows how a mother can, in her suffering, carry the sins of her son. Finally, St. Paul of the Cross reinforces the importance of suffering patiently and bearing within and without the image of Christ crucified by how we suffer.

In her book on Saints for the Sick, Joan Cruz described the lives of a number of saints and holy individuals some of whom offered up their illnesses. By an act of their will they united their sufferings with Christ's suffering for a variety of intentions to include: the Church, missions, sinners, the Pope, clergymen and missionaries. Saint Aldegund (630-684) of France, who suffered from breast cancer, offered her pain and suffering for the salvation of sinners. Servant of God Aldo Blundo (1919-1934) offered his progressive paralysis and nearsightedness followed by a broken leg for the salvation of sinners. When he did not receive a cure at Lourdes, he accepted this and offered his sufferings for wayward youth and for priests. Twenty of the ninety-four holy men and women listed in this anthology specifically offered their pain and suffering for an intention. Silvio Dissegna who suffered from a pain in the leg that was eventually diagnosed as bone cancer offered his suffering one day for the Pope and the Church. On another day he offered it for the clergymen, on another for sinners and yet on another for missionaries. He said, "My vocation is to suffer...I offer my pains with those of Jesus crucified, for the entire world...I must remain with Jesus, the one I have in my heart. Jesus, I suffer like You when You were crucified...I am covering the road to Calvary, and afterward there will be the crucifixion...Jesus wants from me many sufferings and prayers."[57] When reviewing the life of Silvio, Pope St. John Paul II reportedly exclaimed, "Silvio is a beautiful example of an innocent soul who willingly endured pain for the love of God."[58]

In these examples we do not see the effects of "offering up" the suffering. In fact, though Betty had a brief reprieve from her suffering, her daughter Debbie subsequently died. How do we know that offering our sufferings with that of Christ for the salvation of souls works? In another story Archbishop Fulton Sheen shared the actual effects of a wife's redemptive suffering on an atheist husband. The full transcript is at Appendix D which discusses the trials of their marriage. After marriage to a common Catholic girl, the husband decided he was an atheist and ridiculed his wife's religion. In response, she studied her faith and accumulated a Catholic library while he accumulated an atheist one. On her death bed she told him that he would become Catholic and a priest which he thought were the ravings of a dying woman. In his grief after her death he traveled and found himself at a church she had entered on their honeymoon. He felt her calling him in so he entered the church. Within his heart he heard her say, "Go to Lourdes." He went to Lourdes and at the Grotto of Our Lady he had a full and immediate conversion. He did not need to ask, now that I am Catholic, what about the Virgin Mary or the Pope etc. He understood fully. Archbishop Fulton Sheen heard this personal story from Fr. Lisieux, a Dominican priest and widower, whom he met while making a retreat in Belgium. Fr. Lisieux shared with Archbishop Sheen, "Fumbling amidst her papers I discovered her will. And the will stated that in 1905 she asked Almighty God to send her sufficient sufferings to purchase my (her husband's) soul. She had written, "On the day that I die, I shall have paid the price. You will have been bought and paid for." Greater love than this no woman hath that she should lay down her life for her husband. In this example the suffering Mrs. Lisieux offered for her husband supernaturally transformed him through the grace of God. We may never know the effect that our redemptive suffering has in the lives of others but we can "offer up" our suffering and do our part to fill up what is lacking for the sake of His body, the Church.

XIII

Rejoice in hope, be patient in tribulation, be constant in prayer.
Bless those who persecute you; bless and do not curse them.
Romans 12:12 & 14

Betty's Suffering – Part 4

Darrel's sister and her husband arrived on Saturday at
11am. Fourteen hours later, on Sunday at 1am on November 12,
2012, Betty Kaiser died in the arms of her husband. Her
breathing pattern changed. Lying in the bed beside her, he knew
the time had come and scooped her up in his arms his eyes
piercing hers with love. Her eyes, that had not been able to focus
and had been rolling in the sockets, suddenly stared directly into
his with a knowing, loving glance. She took her last breath and
her soul left her body.

Through her suffering and death, Betty brought her husband
Darrel back to Christ. Or perhaps through Darrel's suffering
Christ brought Darrel back to communion with God. Darrel
returned to the church of his childhood and began incorporating
Christian themes into the books he wrote. Had she been killed in
the hospital or her death hastened in their home would this have
occurred?

Betty's suffering was redemptive. It brought her to
baptism. It brought her husband back from a 40 year separation
from Christ. Was Betty specifically "offering up" her suffering
for the salvation of Darrel's soul? No one can know the depth of

another person's heart. However the fruits of her death are apparent. If her life had been ended prematurely, Darrel would have been robbed of learning the true meaning of love. "To love is to find one's greatest good in another."[59] "The happiness of the beloved is the happiness of the lover."[60] In caring for his wife, he exemplified self-giving, self-sacrificing love and he suffered. Darrel died to himself and his needs caring for his wife day and night to the point of extreme exhaustion. As she held on awaiting the return of Darrel's only sister Kathy, Betty also amazing exemplified this love for her husband who'd been her major concern when she was diagnosed and exclaimed, "What about Darrel?" The night Darrel admitted he would administer the morphine suppository was the night that he had finally come to terms with Betty's impending death and was ready to let her go. Now he truly loved his wife, not for his sake, but for hers. He was now willing to let her go. He did, however, continue to care for her until God, in His infinite wisdom and mercy, decided to take her home.

In addition to the spiritual experience Darrel had while lying next to his wife in bed, he also shared one after her death. He did not want to live after Betty died. In fact, the first year was very, very, very difficult. The last lucid statement she made to him occurred suddenly one day when she regained consciousness and clearly stated, "Darrel, you've got to keep writing your novels." She then drifted off to sleep and never spoke again.

After her death, he was in anguish imagining that he could not go on. As he spoke to Betty in spirit, he felt her reach into his chest and squeeze his heart and say, "You have to go on. Darrel you promised!" He felt intense pain and she did not let go until he agreed.

It was a difficult year after Betty's death. Through the suffering of her illness and death, both she and Darrel returned to Christ. After an intense education in the school of suffering, Darrel's insights regarding suffering, following a review of this paper, are in Table 4. Their journey is chronicled by Darrel Kaiser in *The Widower: Our Story of God's Grace, Mercy and Blessings*. The final example below describes the difference when a person is appropriately and inappropriately medicated during the dying trajectory.

Table 4. Insight from the School of Suffering
"On a personal level, I do believe that all suffering, whether one means to or not, is added to our Savior's suffering for all of us... as we are all GOD's children, whether we know, admit or acknowledge it; and I believe GOD uses all for our 'Good' out of His unconditional eternal and infinite love, as He chooses for His own reasons. Just my thoughts... ". Darrel Kaiser
Source: Personal communication Oct 25, 2014

XIV

Suffering exists in the world in order to
unleash love in the caregiver.
Pope St. John Paul II

Death of a Father and Father-in-Law

In Appendix E, Shelby Brown describes the death of her father and father-in-law. One died without medication, the other was given opioid analgesics though he did not have physical pain. He had a respiratory condition which would not improve with additional treatment. He was oxygen dependent but was alive and communicating when last seen by his son. Hospice was called into the nursing home to assist in his care. After administering several doses of opioid analgesics, he became sedated, was not able to eat or drink and died in three days. The daughter-in-law wrote the narrative sharing the difference between the two deaths. In the first one her father saw a vision of his son who'd died previously. This gave his wife much relief and both wife and daughter a firm faith in life after death. In the second instance there was no spiritual experience and the son and daughter-in-law felt cheated.

This last example shows how suffering born patiently in love can redeem others as they glimpse across the veil, while hastening death may serve to rob families of this opportunity as well as the opportunity for the living to say their last goodbyes and resolve unresolved issues. Finally, we can only speculate what prematurely ending someone's life, thereby ending any chance of salutatory repentance, does to the soul and salvation of each person.

CONCLUSION

Everyone's life journey is different. However, each ones suffering can build up the Body of Christ by uniting their suffering and daily inconveniences with Christ's passion and death. "It is only when offered up in union with Christ's redemptive act that our suffering has purpose and that God is able to make use of our anguish and pain for the good of others and for the salvation of the world."[61] In a recent CD, Jason Evert summarized the theology of suffering reflecting on Colossians 1:24:

> Jesus didn't suffer so you would not have to suffer. Jesus suffered so you would know how to suffer. And the theology behind this is that upon the cross Jesus sufficiently merited all of the graces of redemption for mankind and if we suffer with Him we can participate in the distribution of those graces to all of mankind. And any suffering He has redeemed. It doesn't matter if it is unemployment, marital problems, or cancer. It doesn't matter what it is, any suffering, He has redeemed. And you can offer it up. And there is great spiritual value in that. John Paul II knew this. A priest came to him once with a broken leg and he joked with the Pope and he said I broke my leg in a skiing accident will you bless my leg. John Paul looked at him and said, "Don't waste your suffering." And he smacked him. And he blessed him, of course, after he smacked him. But don't waste your suffering.[62]

This paper has described redemptive suffering while chronicling the life and death of Betty who, with her husband of forty years, allowed me to accompany her on her end-of-life journey and first hand understand the value of suffering and observe its redeeming effect. Much suffering occurs in this life. Suffering is part of the Christian life. The Christian is called to pick up their cross daily dying to self, to self-indulgence, self-worship and self-exaltation. This suffering can be wasted or it can be patiently united in love with Christ suffering on the cross and help build up the Body of Christ. Suffering endured patiently and united by an act of the will to Christ's suffering on the cross can bring great graces into the world and help redeem mankind. This action can be done with both little and great suffering. May we "offer up" our daily trials to build up Christ's body, the Church, and participate with Him in redeeming the world.

BIBLIOGRAPHY

Allen, Sr, Prudence. *Christian Anthropology Parts I and II.* Denver: ENDOW (Educating on the Nature and Dignity of Women), 2009.

Angelica, Mother M. *The Healing Power of Suffering.* Birmingham, AL: Eternal Word Television Network, Inc. Catholic Publisher, 1977.

Aquinas, St. Thomas. *Catena Aurea: Gospel of John.* Edited by John Henry Newman. Boonville, New York: Preserving Christian Publications, 2009.

Aquinas, St. Thomas. "Commentary on the Colossians." Priory of the Immaculate Conception. Edited by O.P. Fabian R. Larcher. Magi Books, Inc. http://dhspriory.org/thomas/english/SSColossians.htm#16 (accessed August 17, 2014).

Augustine, St. Aurelius. In *The Liturgy of the Hours: IV-Ordinary Time Weeks 18-34* revised by Decree of the Second Vatican Ecumenical Council and published by authority of Pope Paul VI, 425. New York: Catholic Book Publishing Corporation, 1975.

Augustine, St. Aurelius. *The Confessions*, Vol 5 of *Great Books of the Western World. Chicago: Encyclopaedia Britannica, Inc., 1984.*

Barclay, William. "The Letter to the Philippians, Colossians and Thessalonians." *The New Daily Study Bible.* Louisville, KY: Westminister John Knox Press, 2003.

Benedict XVI, Pope. *Spe Salvi (On Christian Hope).* Vatican library online. 30 November 2007, accessed 9 March 2015. Available from: http://w2.vatican.va/content/benedictxvi/en/encyclicals/documents/hf_ben-xvi_enc_20071130_spe-salvi.html.

Bland, Betty. *Debbie.* Personal unpublished narrative. Huntsville, Alabama, 2014.

Brown, Raymond, Joseph Fitzmyer and Roland Murphy. *The Jerome Bible Commentary*. Englewood Cliffs, NJ: Prentice Hall Inc., 1968.

Brown, Raymond, Joseph Fitzmyer, and Roland Murphy. *The New Jerome Bible Commentary*. Upper Saddle River, NJ: Prentice Hall, 1990.

Brown, Shelby. *Hospice*. Personal unpublished narrative. Huntsville, Alabama, 2013.

Cassell, Eric. "The relationship between pain and suffering." In *Advances in Pain Research and Therapy*, edited by C. Stratton Hill Jr. and William s. Fields, 61-70, New York: Raven Press, 1989. *11 (*1989): 61-70.

Catholic Truth Society. *The CTS New Catholic Bible*. London: The Incorporated Catholic Truth Society, 2007.

Cavins, Jeff. *Walking towards Eternity: Daring to Walk the Walk.* CD #7. West Chester, PA: Ascension Press, 2013.

Cavins, Jeff and Matthew Pinto. *Amazing Grace for Those Who Suffer: 10 Life Changing Stories of Hope and Healing.* West Chester, Pennsylvania: Ascension Press, 2002.

Clausewitz, General Carl von. *On War.* Translated by Colonel J.J. Graham. https://edcat.uni-muenster.de/.../Clausewitz%20%22On%20 War%22.pdf (accessed October 25, 2014) London, 1874.

Chrysostom, John. "Chrysostom: Homilies on Galatians, Ephesians, Philippians, Colossians, Thessalonians, Timothy, Titus and Philemon." In *Nicene and Post Nicene Fathers.* Edited by Philip Schaff, Vol 13, Peabody, MA: Hendrickson Publishers, 1889.

Cruz, Joan Carroll. *Saints for the Sick: Heavenly Help for Those Who Suffer*. Charlotte, North Carolina: TAN Books, 2010.

Denton, Jeremiah. *Walking Through the Valley of the Shadow of Death.* CD-ROM. Grand Rapids, MI: Lighthouse Catholic Media, 2014.

Denton, Jeremiah. *When Hell was in Session,* Washington, D.C.: WorldNetDaily, 1998.

Division of Christian Education of the National Council of Churches of Christ. *The Holy Bible*, Revised Standard Version-Second Catholic Edition. San Francisco, Ignatius Press, 2006 *(unless otherwise noted, Scripture texts are from the RSV-CE)*.

Dreher, Rod. *How Dante Can Save Your Life: The Life-Changing Wisdom of History's Greatest Poem.* New York: Regan Arst, 2015.

Droste, Sr. Catherine Joseph, Madelyn Winstead and Terry Polakovic. *Setting the World Ablaze: St. Catherine of Siena.* Denver: ENDOW (Educating on the Nature and Dignity of Women). 2014.

Dubuc, Jean-Guy. *Brother André: Friend of the Suffering,* Apostle of Saint Joseph. Notre Dame, Indiana: Ave Maria Press, 1999.

Duportal, Marguerite. *How to Make Sense of Suffering.* Manchester, New Hampshire: Sophia Institute Press, 2005.

EWTN. "Fr. Tyson Wood-2014-6-16-Former Lutheran." The Journey Home (accessed October 19, 2014) http://www.youtube.com/watch?v=NGUfjtfKU7o&sns=em

Evert, Jason. *Parenting for Purity.* CD. Lighthouse Catholic Media, 2013.

The English College at Douay. *The Holy Bible*: Douay-Rheims Version, First Published By the English College at Douay, A.D. OT 1609, NT 1582; Translated from the Latin Vulgate: Diligently Compared with the Hebrew, Greek and Other Editions in Diverse Languages. Charlotte, NC: Saint Benedict Press, 2009.

Frankl, Viktor E. *Man's Search for Meaning.* Boston: Beacon Press, 2006.

Hahn, Scott. *Hope for Hard Times*. Huntington, Indiana: Our Sunday Visitor, Inc., 2009.

Hahn, Scott. *Ignatius Catholic Study Bible-New Testament Revised Standard Version, 2nd Catholic Edition*. San Francisco: Ignatius Press, 2001.

Houselander, Caryll. *This War Is the Passion*. New York: Sheed & Ward, 1941. (Reprinted by Ave Maria Press, Notre Dame, 2008).

International Association for the Study of Pain (IASP). Taxonomy: Pain. http://www.iasppain.org/Taxonomy?navItem Number=576#Pain (accessed October 23, 2014).

Isajiw, George. Medical education in the shadow of 'stealth euthanasia' among Catholics: Are we fighting secularism or heresy? *The Linare Quarterly* 82 (3) 2015, 210-216.

John Paul II, Pope Saint. *Laborem Excercens (On Human Work)*. Vatican library online 14 September 1981, accessed 10 March 2015. Available from: http://w2.vatican.va/ content/john-paul-ii/en/encyclicals/documents/hf_jpii_enc_14091981_laboremexercens.html.

John Paul II, Pope Saint. *Salvifici Doloris (On the Christian Meaning of Human Suffering)*. Vatican library online. 11 February 1984, accessed 10 March 2015. Available from: http://w2.vatican.va/content/john-paul-ii/en/apost_letters/1984/documents/hf_jp-ii_apl_11021984_salvifici-doloris.html

Kaiser, Darrel. *Widower: Our Story of God's Grace, Mercy and Blessings*. Huntsville, Alabama: Green Mountain, 2013.

Kane, John A. *How to Make a Good Confession*. Manchester, New Hampshire: Sophia Institute, 2001.

Kheriaty, Aaron and Fr. John Cihak. *The Catholic Guide to Depression: How the Saints, the Sacraments, and Psychiatry Can Help You Break Its Grip and Find Happiness Again.* Manchester, New Hampshire: Sophia Institute Press, 2012.

Kreeft, Peter. *Making Sense Out of Suffering.* Cincinnati: St Anthony Messenger Press, 1986.

Kowalska, Saint Maria Faustina. *Divine Mercy in My Soul: Diary of Saint Maria Faustina Kowalska.* Stockbridge, Massachusetts: Marian Press, 2011.

Leen, Edward. *Why the Cross?* New Rochelle, NY: Scepter, 1938.

Marmion, Dom Columba. *Suffering with Christ: An Anthology of Writings of Dom Columba Marmion*, O.S.B. compiled by Dom Raymund Thibaut, O.S.B. Westminster, Maryland: The Newman Press, 1952.

McCaffery, Margo. *Nursing Practice Theories Related to Cognition, Bodily Pain, and Man-Environment Interactions.* Los Angeles: University of California at Los Angeles Students' Store, 1968.

Morice, Father Henri. *Why Bad Things Happen to Good Catholic: And Other Mysteries of God's Love and Providence – Explained!* Manchester, New Hampshire: Sophia Institute Press, 2002.

Mother Teresa of Calcutta. Presentation at the Cathedral of St. Mary of the Assumption. Personal Audiocassette. San Francisco, CA, 1982.

National Catholic Bioethics Center (NCBC). *A Catholic Guide to End-of-Life Decisions: An Explanation of Church Teaching on Advnce Directives, Euthanasia and Physician-Assisted Suicide.* Philadelphia: NCBC, 2011.

Navarre University Faculty of Theology. *The Navarre Bible, Gospes & Acts.* 2nd ed. New York: Scepter Publishers, 2008.

Navarre University Faculty of Theology. *The Navarre Bible, Revelation and Hebrews and Catholic Letters.* New York: Scepter Publishers, 2006.

Navarre University Faculty of Theology. *The Navarre Bible, The Letters of Saint Paul.* 2nd ed. New York: Sceptor Publishers, 2008.

Navarre, Faculty of Theology of the University of. *The Navarre Bible: New Testament.* Edited by Brian McCarthy, Thomas McGovern and James Gavigan. New York: Scepter Publishers, 2008.

O'Sullivan, Fr. Paul. *How to Make the Greatest Evil in Our Lives Our Greatest Happiness.* Holy Wounds Apostolate, P.O. Box 227, Wisconsin Rapids, WI 54435. www.holywoundsapostolate.com

Paul of the Cross, Saint. In *The Liturgy of the Hours: IV-Ordinary Time Weeks 18-34* revised by Decree of the Second Vatican Ecumenical Council and published by authority of Pope Paul VI, Pope. 1505-1506. New York: Catholic Book Publishing Corporation, 1975.

Paz, Cesar Alejandro Mora. 1998. Colossians. In *The International Bible Commentary,* ed. William R. Farmer, 1703. Collegeville, MN: The Liturgical Press.

Ratzinger, Joseph. *Jesus of Nazareth, The Illustrated Edition.* Vatican City: Libreria Editrice Vaticana, 2008.

Rose of Lima, Saint. In *The Liturgy of the Hours: IV-Ordinary Time Weeks 18-34* revised by Decree of the Second Vatican Ecumenical Council and published by authority of Pope Paul VI, 1342-1343. New York: Catholic Book Publishing Corporation, 1975.

Schroeder, Robert G. *John Paul II and the Meaning of Suffering: Lessons from a Spiritual Master.* Huntington, IN, Our Sunday Visitor, Inc. 2008.

Selner-Wright, Susan. *Aquinas for Beginners: An Introduction to the Scholarly Saint and his Extraordinary Works.* West Chester, PA: Ascension Press, 2007.

Selner-Wright, Susan. *Aquinas for Beginners, Part 2.* West Chester, PA: Ascension Press, 2010.

Shaw, Russell. *Does Suffering Make Sense?* New York: Scepter Publishers, 2000

Sheen, Venerable Archbishop Fulton J. *Calvary and the Mass: The Consecration.* Cannons Regular of St. John Cantius, Sancta Missa online, 2010, accessed 23 October 2015. Available from: http://www.sanctamissa.org/en/resources/books/calvary/the-consecration.html.

Sheen, Venerable Archbishop Fulton J. *Life is Worth Living.* CD-ROM. Sycamore, IL: Lighthouse Catholic Media, NFP, 2014.

United States Catholic Conference Inc.---Libreria Editrice Vaticana. *Catechism of the Catholic Church.* 2nd ed. Washington, D.C.: United States Catholic Conference, Inc., 1997.

Upchurch, Catherine, Irene Nowell and Ronald Witherup. *Little Rock Catholic Study Bible* Collegeville, MN: Liturgical Press, 2011.

Van der Sloot, Sharon. *Salvifici Doloris: A Study Guide for The Apostolic Letter of Pope John Paul II On the Christian Meaning of Human Suffering.* Denver: ENDOW, 2008.

Van Zeller, Dom Hubert. *Suffering: The Catholic Answer. The Cross of Christ and Its Meaning for You.* Manchester, New Hampshire: Sophia Institute Press, 2002.

Weinandy, Thomas G. *Does God Suffer?* Notre Dame, Indiana: University of Notre Dame Press, 2000.

APPENDICES

Appendix A - Mother Teresa of Calcutta

"One day I met a lady who was dying of cancer, most terrible pain. And I said to her, Know this pain, this suffering is but a kiss of Jesus, a sign that you have come so close to Him on the cross that He can kiss you. And the lady joined her hands and said, 'Mother Teresa, please tell Jesus to stop kissing me.' So beautiful **because suffering is a gift of God. It is a sign that we have come so close to Him that we can share His passion, that we can share the joy of loving with Him in pain, in suffering. Suffering is not a punishment; suffering is a gift, a gift that purifies us, that sanctifies us**. It's really the kiss of Jesus. And I think today when the world is suffering so much, so much... I feel that the passion of Christ is being relived in our people.

So let us pray. Let us make sacrifices. Let us be to each other that joy, that love, that compassion. Let us allow God to love through us today. God loves the world very much and he wants to prove his love through us, through you, through me. So let us love each other as He loves each one of us. My prayer for you will be that you grow in holiness that you grow in the likeness of Christ through this love for each other. Doesn't matter color, doesn't matter place, doesn't matter cost, doesn't matter religion, doesn't matter, He's there to give us the joy, the strength, the love and He wants us to love as He has loved each one of us. And you pray for us that we may not spoil God's work, that it remains His, His and that we together we really do something beautiful for God. God bless you."[63]

Mother Teresa, (1910-1997)
Cathedral of St. Mary of the Assumption
San Francisco, California, 1982

Appendix B - Helping Jesus Carry the Cross from Betty Bland

October 23, 2014

Dear Diana,

Hope this isn't too late for you. Had to take Charles to a movie and then had a lectors meeting and just got home.

In 1983 or 84 at the beginning of Lent we began having a very difficult time with Debbie. Her personality completely changed. She was a straight A student and began making F's

Larry had retired in May 83 & we moved to Madison. Debbie wanted to live on the Arsenal. And every day she complained.

It was the 1st or 2nd day of lent and Debbie went somewhere with a *new* friend. I sat up waiting for her to come home. About 3 a.m. I was looking out front. Across the street there are woods and at the one end, two dogwoods were almost entwined. They were growing very close together. As I was praying (thought she had been injured in an accident) I was looking at those two trees. **All of a sudden I saw the face of Jesus in the trees.** He looked like how he is pictured on Veronica's Veil. I had been crying because I was so frightened that she had not come home yet. I thought I am seeing things, wiped my eyes and suddenly an inner feeling or voice said to me, **"You are going to have to help me carry my cross"**. She came home about 7 a.m.

I told Larry what had happened. Every night for the rest of Lent I saw Jesus. I asked Larry if he saw him too. He said he thought he saw something but didn't know if it was Jesus face.

For over 2 years we lived a nightmare. We never knew where she was or what she would do next. I don't remember those two years. I don't remember any local events. Someone told me there was a terrible train wreck on Governor's drive. I don't remember.

One day I got a prank call. Someone said they were from Bob Jones [*High School*] and Debbie wasn't at school. **That's when I asked God to please take this burden away from us – we just couldn't take any more. He did lessen the burden for several weeks** and then problems began again.

We had so many heartaches until she passed away. She was living in North Carolina at the time and in a Baptist Hospital. I demanded that a priest come and give her last rites. Finally they consented to call a priest from St. Leo's Parish. She was 21 years old and died from meningitis and cardiac failure. Charles was 2 at the time and we raised him since.

Hope this is what you need. I think I could write a book about all the things that happened to her and to us.

Blessings,
Betty

Appendix C – Admiral Jeremiah Denton, POW, Vietnam

In his presentation on the Lighthouse Catholic Media CD, *"Walking through the Valley of the Shadow of Death,"* Admiral Jeremiah Denton shared the power of prayer during times of torture and despair during the 7 years and 7 months he was held as a POW in North Vietnam (1965-1973). *"The more you are forced to pray the more you get answers, the more you go to God the more He is with you."*[64] The following are two examples of the power of prayer and suffering from the CD.

"So, for a lot of reasons, we were tougher than we thought we could be or than they thought we could be. And prayer had everything to do with that... Only very occasionally did they try to get operational information from us. It was mostly just the propaganda motive as I've mentioned before. Mainly because there were no long range plans in that war. What were they going to get from me? I didn't know what they were going to do the next day. What could they ask me? In a very few cases that was done in special cases during the war but it's almost not worth mentioning. A few times they came at us for operational information that affected the thing they hated the worst and that was the integrity of our command and control of our own people. And it was the first example of the power of prayer that I will offer you that is personal. It was in a situation like that. I had already been tortured in January and in April for a biography and a confession. Now in the fall of the year after I was shot down I was being tortured for information about communications in our camp. I was running that camp. The only thing I was kind of good at was communications. I liked games and I invented a lot of things we used for communication some of which would impress you, not because I'm smart but because God answered prayers. When you say, "Teach me a way, inspire me with a method." And we had plenty. And it went through one chapter after another. They'd introduce a counter measure, we'd introduce another measure for which they had to come up with a counter measure. We had all kinds of codes, we had all kinds of methods. But I knew it all. And not only would I have betrayed the means by which we were keeping us together and set up back a long way. But they would have been able to credibly tell the rest of the camp on the radio and in interrogations that Denton broke and here is what he said... And they would know that they were telling the truth. So I wasn't about to give them anything.

[Describes the torture] And the rig entailed a wooden palate. And at that end my legs were flat and my hands were tied, in what they called, in hell cuffs behind me. And there was a bar underneath my legs with two shackles over my legs with rope arranged so that the shackles pressed down on my legs forcing the Achilles tendon area into the bar. And there was a pulley arrangement by which the guards could tighten that up as they saw fit. In that arrangement, your legs go quite fast. I had no pain in my legs maybe after 3 hours. But the pain in the back... You can't lie back with hell cuffs on. There's no way you could lie back. It just tears your wrists and the bone and just twists it. It's impossible. So you sit there and with no meat on your butt, your spine resting on the wooden thing, your back, trying to find a way to get comfortable, in five days and five nights it hurts a lot and it changes the way it hurts. So I was hurting a lot so I thought, "Well, I'm far enough gone." I wasn't eating or drinking. "I'll say, '*Bao cao,*'" meaning, "I surrender," and give then some stuff they already know. And knowing how close I am to dying they will come off me, accept what I give them and all's well... *[He gave them information they already knew]*

I thought they were going to let me go. But they didn't. They put me back into the rig. And that surprised me and depressed me. And after running out of every prayer, rehearsed memorized prayer and every prayer that I could think up. Any kind of work of reason that I could present to God, **I reached the point where I could not think any more except to say to God, *"I have done all I can find able in myself to do and I'm turning the whole thing over to You. You have it."* To me what happened was, it would be self-serving to say a miracle.** But I had been alternating between shaking from chills, which might last 10 minutes and you could hear my irons and cuffs all over the camp. It was 2 or 3 o'clock in the morning AND no sweating, because I had exhausted all the liquid from my body but being very, very hot. **And at that moment that I offered that surrender I was in the midst of a chill. In one instance, my mind, well first my body, became warm like the most blessed comforter had been placed over me. What had been pain, fear, anxiety, almost despair became the greatest composure I have ever experienced in my life. I knew that there was nothing in this world that could be applied to me to hurt me, my spirit or my body.** Having established my humility... And within a few minutes the guards came to the door a little bit anxious because I had been a long time and they had started telling the officers, I learned later, that I was going to die and they were not getting anywhere with me. And the man we uncharitably called the lump. He had a tumor on his forehead. And he was an expert in torture and in psychology. The camp commander stood outside the door and told him, break his legs off but make him break. Well they came in, the two guards, one of them was somewhat of a brute. The other was a young man about 18 or 19 we called Smiley, a wonderful young man. Who just did his duty and didn't like it very much. And he and this guy got on the rope. **And I just looked at Smiley and he looked at me and he saw in my face what I told you I felt. And his face contorted instantly. He dragged the other guy off the ropes and went out and started screaming at the officer. This is foolish. There's nothing you are going to get out of this man. I won't do it anymore.** And so I didn't give them anything, not a face saving thing. And shortly they came in, fixed up the places on my leg where the iron, rust and stuff had gotten in. My Achilles tendons were eaten in 3/8". …. [described injuries]. I am just telling you the power of prayer.

Another example of the power of prayer: "About a year later, just before moving to the place that was so small, cramped. They were having a torture purge in another camp, the main prison, the Hanoi Hilton that you may have heard about. And I was getting very near despair. They used to call me the president of the optimist club because I liked to try to uplift everybody and I can usually see a brighter side to things. But I was near despair. I had a number of times prayed to die in the torture rig but I had never without that approached despair until then. I could hear men screaming being tortured. It was the summer of 1967. It was the worst time for going after operational information. There were 10 or so examples about that. And if you get 2 or more men from the same plane and they lie and you make them say something and then you keep working on them until they get down to the last little part it's kind of sad, generally they can force something out of them. I could hear the screaming. It was quiet. I could not communicate. They had a guard leaning up against my door. He could hear me breathe. He could hear that kind of a tap. And I prayed that there be a cease to the torture. I prayed that I would develop a means of communication that would work even under those circumstances. Both things came true much later, but they came true. **But during that time of near despair I just said, "Lord I don't know what to do. I don't know what to say. I don't know how to pray about this."** And I've always had this problem that many of you might have about resolving, "Work as though everything depends on you. Pray as though everything depends on God." Maybe that's not a conflicting statement but sometimes it occurs to me as one. And I tried to do it. Me do it. I can't do it. And I often have trouble with the balance. And I was lying there absolutely quite, totally alert, in irons. My cell mate Jim Mulligan was down below and he was asleep **and I heard in the absolute quiet the most beautifully modulated male voice from a distance of like 8 feet from me. If you can imagine the silence in a concrete cell. "'Say Sacred Heart of Jesus, I give myself to you.'" I was never awed more before or since in my life.** I was sure Mulligan had heard it. I thought it would wake him up. I said, "Jim, did you hear that?" He stirred and said, "What?" So I knew he hadn't heard it. But you know, I can't prove it. I just tell you that's what happened. And I have never had a day, rarely an hour go by that I don't say that."[65]

This is an excerpt from the Lighthouse Catholic Media CD, "*Walking through the Valley of the Shadow of Death*," This and other excellent Lighthouse Catholic Media CDs are available at

Appendix D - Is Christianity Easy? Venerable Archbishop Fulton Sheen

Really when we get down to rock bottom, what are we afraid of? We are afraid to give our failure to God because we fear that he may take our head. So we have little secret gardens back in our heart that we tend. The fruit is not His. It's ours. We wall it off from Him. Sometimes a petty sin or a vice or selfishness, whatever it happens to be. We do not get the full joy of being a Christian. It's very hard for an egg, for example, to turn into a bird. But it would be much harder for it to learn to fly while remaining an egg. We are just like eggs now. And we cannot go on being just what we call a good egg. If we insist on just being a good egg, we either become a good egg, a really good one or a bad one. And what is a good egg? A good egg is an egg that hatches. It can be readily seen that **what our Blessed Lord insists upon is a kind of a death.** Namely we have to renew in our own lives exactly what happened in His. He is the pattern. He repeatedly said to, not only to Nicodemas, but to us, if we are to live again, we have to perish to that old existence. If there is anybody who hopes that in Christ the real danger spots are rendered harmless and that nothing else can happen to us because after all He's what we call a kind savior and who takes even hardened sinners back with no questions asks. Well that person must first come to terms with the text that Our Blessed Lord said He would not subtract not one jot or tittle from the severity of God's law, that He had come not to abolish the law but to perfect it. In other words, grace is not cheap. It cost Our Lord His life. Can you think of anything that is more costly than that for which a man must pay on a cross? So if we want peace, we have to pay that price, without that death to the lower life, not the death to our higher life, no, but without that death to our lower life, there's no peace. There's only fear and we live just a kind of a half existence. Remember our Blessed Lord said that, *"He who wills to do the will of the Father in heaven will know whether the teaching is from God."* By this He means that one of the reasons there are agnostics and skeptics is because they're not keeping the law of God. If we know His will, we will understand His doctrine. It could very well be that we have entirely too much insistence upon a knowledge of Christian doctrine and not enough insistence upon doing. Our Blessed Lord never said that if you know My doctrine, you will do My will. But He did say that, *"If you do My will, you will know My doctrine."* In other words, only he who does the will, who is in earnest about it, who stakes his life on it, will come to understand Christ and all that His redemption means. Our Lord is known really only to those who venture, not to the cowards is He known.

Now at first Our Blessed Lord is always a disturber. When you are still living in the natural order, Oh, He seems to irritate you. You're dealing with a God who seems to be leading you into a kind of crucifixion. You are a nice, easy going worldling and you have settled down comfortably into what you call your world view. But if you are in earnest with Christ, you will have to give up that comfort. And not because you are supposed to be a nervous worrier, but simply because it is a false peace. The first advent, therefore, of Christ into our lives is actually that of one who upsets us. But then once we give ourselves to Him, He becomes our defender. Before we have Christ our heart accuses us. Then after we give ourselves to Our Lord and His law of love then our heart is at peace and Christ becomes our defender. His attitude completely changes once we have changed ours. This is just another way of putting the difference between commandments and love. Commandments only restrain me. We see them as hurdles and obstacles in the way of life. And those who live by the commandments ask, "How far can I go? What is the limit? How close can I get to the abyss without tumbling in? Is it a mortal sin?" This is not the way of love. It's not the way of peace. It is the old Adam that is within me that talks this way about commands. So when I merely obey commands, I am never there as a whole person but perhaps at most with only the better half of myself and the other half remains in opposition. That's the psychological state of everyone who obeys a command, never the whole heart. But when I love, I am a whole person. For love is a movement of my whole self. It is an overflowing limitless giving of oneself. Therefore it can never be commanded. It can only happen.

Up to this point we have said that the Christian doctrine of morality is a total commitment to Christ so that we put on His mind; we think His thoughts; we love what He loves; and we ask ourselves whenever we do anything, will this be pleasing to Him. But there's another side to the love of God, is the love of neighbor. The two laws go together. And the love of neighbor is not merely giving eggs to the neighbor when the neighbor wishes it. It is really being a "sin bearer." What does that mean? Well so years ago I remember meeting a woman who was very much distressed because her son had been put into prison. I think it was the 4th arrest for crime, robbery, and murder. She was bitterly ashamed and brokenhearted. And then I asked myself, "Why does she have all this shame?" **And there came to me the words of the Prophet Isaiah said that referred to Our Lord. And I might say of her, she had born his griefs, carried his sorrows and the chastisement of his peace was upon her and it would only be by her stripes that he would be healed. This good mother had very few sins in her life, certainly no serious sins and yet love made her exceedingly sinful for his sake. So immediately the mystery cleared up. The love with which a woman can put out for her son and which makes her so entirely one with him, that his sin is her sin, his disgrace is her disgrace, his shame is her shame is the nearest thing that we can ever get on this earth to the love of God and to know what God did.** In our own turn therefore, we have to see that all of our sins became His sins, our disgrace was His disgrace, our shame, His shame. **And in His own body He bear our sins upon the tree.** This is what forgiveness costs. That's why we said grace is not easy. We are not therefore to think that we are pious when we begin living our individual holy lives apart from our neighbor and apart from the world and suffering humanity. That was the trouble with Simon the Pharisee. The sinful woman came into the house and poured out ointment upon the feet of Our Blessed Lord. Simon was scandalized. He wanted no contact with anyone that was sinful. He was only concerned about keeping the law just for himself and maybe his own false and inner peace. And Our Blessed Lord said to Simon, "Do you see this woman? Do you understand her? Her sins are part of the sins of the world. And then He went on to say that He was taking on her sins and the pouring of the ointment was a preparation for His crucifixion and His burial. She was forgiven much and forgiveness costs an awful lot.

Forgiveness is love in action and love means sin bearing. Forgiveness can only be accomplished by sin bearing. And sin bearing means a cross. It means that to God and it must mean that to us. That is why our Blessed Lord said to us, *"If any man will be my disciple, let him take up his cross and follow me."* The means of the cross is love bearing the sin of the beloved because of oneness with him. We can know the sin bearer Christ only as we bear the sins of others. We are redeemed in order to be redeemers. And we are not saved until God makes us saviors. The Christian has to go with Our Lord into the Garden of Gethsemane and must pass from there to Calvary **filling up in his**

body what is lacking in the sufferings of Christ for His body's sake which is the Church. We cannot like Pilate wash our hands and say I'm innocent of the blood of the world, and innocent of the sufferings of the world. The Church is a Church in deed. It is a body of sin bearing people, people who love with the love of God that is shed abroad in their hearts. They are a body of people who can forgive because they have been forgiven; who have loved, therefore they can become lovers. Unless the Church of Christ is by love so united with the whole of mankind, the sin of the world is the sin of the Church, the disgrace of the world is the disgrace of the Church, the shame of the world, the shame of the Church, the poverty of the world, the poverty of the Church, then it is no Church at all. The Church is not, and never can be, an end in itself. It is a means of salvation for the world. Not just our own sanctification. We cannot save ourselves alone. We pray in the context of Our Father, not my father. Our daily bread, not my daily bread. The Church is the agent of salvation for all mankind. It is not a refuge of peace. It is an army preparing for war. We seek security but only in sacrifice and this is the mark of the Church and the hallmark of the cross itself. And if the sin of our modern slums and the degradation that they cause, if the sin of our overcrowded rotten houses and the ugliness and vice they bring, if the sin of unemployment with the damnation of body and soul that it means to men and women; if the sin of the heartless, thoughtless luxury at one end standing out against the squalid poverty of Africa, Asia and Latin America at the other. If the sin of commercial trickery and dishonesty and the whole sale defrauding of the poor, if the sin of prostitution and the murder of women and children by disease, and if the sin of war, the very sins which is but the bursting and the festering of all the filth that others have bread in years of miscalled peace, if all of that is not laid upon the Church as a burden and upon us as members of the Church. And if we do not feel it, we are not worthy members of the Church. We have missed our vocation. This is Christian morality, not just the keeping of the commandments. It's love, total commitment and it's taking upon ourselves the sins of others. This is the new law. Love God, Love your neighbor (bold mine).

This is an excerpt from the Lighthouse Catholic Media CD, "*Life is Worth Living*," This and other excellent CDs are available at http://www.lighthousecatholicmedia.org/.

Appendix E - The Problem of Love, Venerable Archbishop Fulton Sheen

The following is a transcript from the Lighthouse Catholic Media CD recording of the Venerable Archbishop Fulton J. Sheen, *Life is Worth Living*. Archbishop Sheen discusses the trials of marriage and then shares the actual supernatural effects of a wife's redemptive suffering on her atheist husband.

It is very often assumed that life should be without trials and difficulties. Our Blessed Lord did not predict it so. He said, "In this world you shall have tribulation." Even when one enters into a realm of love, such as marriage, there are trials and difficulties. And it is those that we would consider in this particular lesson. This is what might be called a "what to do kit" when there are difficulties in marriage. We shall consider two.

First when marriage dulls. Second when the other partner becomes, what is sometimes said, "impossible."

First when marriage dulls. Now this it does simply because everything in life does after a time. Love does not continue to be one abiding ecstasy. Simply because flesh is the medium of marriage love it suffers the penalty of the flesh. It becomes used to affection. As life goes on a greater stimulus is required to produce an equal reaction to sensation. The eye can soon become used to beauty. The fingers used to the touch of a friend. The intimacy which was first so desirable could become at times a burden. There is such a thing as, "I want to be alone feeling" or "I think that I will go home to mother feeling." And these strip the eye of rose colored glasses. Bills begin to come into the kitchen and love is in the danger of walking out of the parlor. The very habit of love becomes boring because it is a habit and not an adventure. It is conceivable that there might even be a yearning for a new partner. Then there comes with children multiplied accidents and diseases and all of this tends to bring down the vision from the clouds, the very realistic visitations to the nursery and sooner or later the affective emotion life is brought face to face with this question. Is love a snare, a delusion? Does it promise what it cannot give? I thought this would be complete happiness. And yet it has settled down to a routine. Now at this point those who think that love is an evolution from the beast, not a gift of God, falsely believe that if they had another partner that other partner could supply what is presently lacking. No that is a fallacy because it forgets that the emptiness does not come from the other partner but from the very nature of life itself. Now here is the reason for that feeling. The heart was made for the Infinite. Only the Infinite can satisfy it. This first ecstasy of love was given to a couple was given to remind them that love was a gift that came from heaven and only by working towards heaven would they ever really discover it to be infinite. Remember when Our Lord gave bread at Capernaum and then later on gave the bread of the Eucharist, the bread of everlasting life, His very self? He was using the bread that He gave to their stomach as a kind of bait to make them become interested in the bread of life, the Eucharist. ...To the human love that God gives us is a bait. It is a kind of a divine come on in order that we might seek the flame which is God. When married life becomes dull, one has not hit the bottom of life. One has only hit the bottom of one's ankle. There's a world of difference between the two. One has not hit the bottom of his soul but only the bottom of his instinct; not the bottom of his mind, but only the bottom of his emotional life. The aforementioned trials are merely so many contacts with reality that God sends into every life. If life went on as a dream without any shock of disillusionment who would ever attain perfect happiness? Who would ever want God? The majority of men would rest in mediocrity if there were not this push on for the perfect love. Acorns are not content to be saplings, children have to grow up and our love has to grow up. Therefore God keeps something back, namely Himself in eternity. If He did not, we would never push forward. Therefore he makes us every now and then run up against a brick wall. In such a crisis we begin to feel our non-entity. We've got an overwhelming sense of nothingness, loneliness. And then if we look at it rightly we see that this life is only a bridge to eternity. The crisis of nothingness has caused the meeting of a fancied ideal and reality, of love as the ego fancies it and as love as it really is. No, love is not a snare. God is not mocking us. And it must not be thought either that this sense of nothingness that comes over marriage, and dullness, is peculiar to marriage itself. It happens in the spiritual life too. We who are dedicated to God as priests and others, brothers and nuns and contemplatives, they all reach this crisis. Prayers become dry and formal. There's danger that we may become used to touching the bread of life. There is not the same emotional thrill in reading mass when one is ordained 40 years as there is at the first mass. There may not be that same ecstasy in visiting the sick when one is ordained 50 years as there was a thrill on the first sick call. And the nun who is teaching children for 30 or 40 years has to bring herself with an extra prayer to realize that all those youngsters have been put before her as charges by almighty God. It becomes difficult for all of us to meditate. Thanksgivings are apt to become shorter after mass. So we have our problem too. It's a problem of love. How can I love better? How can I pray better? How can I establish greater union with God?

The answer is by sacrifices. In as much as we here are not concerned with the development of the spiritual life only with the development of love life in marriage, we return again to marriage. And we say that just as there is such a thing in the spiritual life as the dark night of the soul, so too in marriage there is such a thing as the dark night of the body. And just as the dark night of the soul in the spiritual life needs considerable purification through self-denial in order to reach deeper insights of love, so too in marriage. Whenever there is discontent, God is stirring the waters of the soul. Really He's reminding us that the perfect love for which we crave is not here. We are on the road to it. Just as a mother eagle will throw its young out of the nest in order that they may learn to fly and so too, God in these moments of trial gives wings to our clay feet and this dryness either in the spiritual life or in the married life can be either for salvation or damnation depending on how it is used. There are two kinds of dryness, the one that rots which is the dryness of God without love and there is the dryness which ripens and that is when one goes through the fire and the heat of sacrifice. In therefore these moments of dullness, in this crisis of nothingness, the idea of eternity has to be reintroduced. But there's this difference, in the day of romance the eternal emphasis was on the ego's durability in love, in the ego's durability. In the crisis of nothingness and dullness the eternal element is God, not the ego. Love now says, "I will love you always for you are lovable through eternity for God's sake." You see which love? That love which began with pleasure and self-satisfaction changes into love for God's sake. The other person becomes less than the necessary condition of passion and more the partner of the soul. Our Blessed Lord said that unless the seed fall to the ground and die it will not spring forth into life. Nothing is born to a higher life without a death to a lower one. The heart has its cycle as well as the planets. And the movement of the heart is an upward spiral and not a circle which turns in upon itself. The crisis of nothingness which follows a dream come true needs its purification and its cross. And the cross is not a roadblock on the way to happiness. It is a ladder up which one climbs to the very heaven of love itself. Therefore there's no need of running off to someone to analyze your mental state just because you find life dull. Intensify your love of God and begin to look upon the other partner as a gift of God and then love will not be dull. And then we will see every human creature bathed in that beauty of God's love.

That brings us to this other problem of marriage and trial. Namely when marriage becomes a cross and when as some say, it is impossible. Well in marriage there is, for better or for worse. Sometimes it turns out worse. And that is the problem we are discussing now. Suppose the husband or the wife becomes a chronic invalid or develops antisocial characteristics, becomes a drunkard, bossy. What are we to do? Well, we said we had to regard always the other person as a gift of God. Now sometimes God's gifts are sweet and sometimes God's gifts are bitter. And whether the other person be sweet or bitter, sick or well, young or old, that other person is still a gift of God. If we're selfish we have to get rid of the other partner. Why? Because the other partner is a burden. St. Paul said, "Bear the burden of one another's failings then you will be fulfilling the law of Christ." Now if you object and say, "Well God never intended that anyone should live under such difficulties." The answer is flatly, "Oh yes he does." Did not our Blessed Lord say, "If any man has a mind to come My way, let him renounce himself, take up his cross and follow Me? The man who tries to save his life shall lose it. It is the man who loses his life for My sake that will secure it." We would all like to have tailor made crosses. In other words, we are always willing to take on some mortification and self-denial if we can choose it. But when God chooses it then we say, "Oh no, I cannot take that cross." Why cannot we realize that, what sickness is to an individual, an unhappy marriage may be to a couple, a trial sent by God in order to perfect them spiritually? After all without certain bitter gifts of God many of our spiritual capacities would be undeveloped. Now such a marriage may indeed be martyrdom but at any rate, he's not robbing his own life of honor nor robbing his soul of peace. The acceptance of such trials of marriage is not a sentence to death as some believe. The Soldier is not sentenced to death because he takes the oath to his country. But he admits that he is ready to face death rather than lose honor. An unhappy marriage is not a condemnation to unhappiness. Then here is this verse of scripture which very few people think about which is so important. It is in St. Paul's epistle to the Corinthians, "The unbelieving husband is sanctified by the believing wife. And the unbelieving wife is sanctified by the believing husband." In other words, the merits, the prayers, the suffering, the patience, the meekness of one passes into the other. If for the example the other partner who was an alcoholic, if that partner were sick, would you not take care of him? Suppose he had tuberculosis or a heart attack would you leave him? Now if he has a moral heart attack is he to be abandoned? And by a moral heart attack I mean guilty of any one of the sins that make marriage so very difficult. If there is such a thing as the transfusion of blood from a healthy member of society to a weak member of society, why can there not be and why is there not the transfer of sanctification. A wife can redeem her husband and a husband can redeem the wife.

There is a spiritual communication. It does not have indeed a romantic satisfaction in it but its returns are eternal. And many a husband and wife after infidelities and excesses will find themselves saved on judgment day as the faithful partner never ceased to pour our prayers for his or her salvation. Let me tell you this story to indicate how the merits of one will pass into the merits of the other. At the turn of this century there was married in Paris just an ordinarily good Catholic girl and an unbelieving medical doctor with a name of Lisieux. He promised to respect the faith of his marriage but immediately after marriage tried to break it down. In addition to practicing medicine he became the editor of an anti-clerical atheistic newspaper in Paris. His wife reacted and decided that she would study her faith. So she built a library of apologetics and he built up an atheistic library in the same house. **In May 1905 as she was dying she said to her husband, Felix, when I am dead you will become a Catholic and a Dominican priest.** He said, "Elizabeth, you know my sentiments. I have sworn hatred of the Church and sworn hatred of God and I shall live in that hatred and I shall die in it." **She repeated her words and she passed away. Fumbling amidst her papers he discovered her will. And the will stated that in 1905 she asked Almighty God to send her sufficient sufferings to purchase his soul. And then she added, "On the day that I die, I shall have paid the price. You will have been bought and paid for. Greater love than this no woman hath that she should lay down her life for her husband." He dismissed this as the fancies of a pious woman.** Though he loved his wife, in order to forget his grief he took a trip in the southern part of France. He stopped in front of a church into which his wife, during their honeymoon, had gone for a visit. She seemed to be speaking to him saying, "Go to Lourdes." **He went to Lourdes but he went there as a rank unbeliever. He had written a book against Lourdes proving that miracles were a fraud and**

a superstition. But as he was standing before the grotto of Our Lady he received the gift of faith, so complete, so total that he never had to go through that process of juxtaposition and say, "Well, now that I believe, how will I answer this difficulty or how will I answer that difficulty." He saw all that he had believed in its utter error and stupidity. Well, the conversion of Dr. Lisieux was about as exciting as the news of the bombardment of Reams. **Then time passed, 1924 I made my retreat in a Dominican monastery in Belgium and there four times a day, and 45 minutes each day I made my retreat under and received the spiritual direction of Father Lisieux, Dominican, Catholic and priest who told me this story.** I tell you it is not often that you can make a retreat under a priest who every now and then will say, "As my dear wife Elizabeth said." The moral of the story is love is not here completely and totally. It is in God. And by loving God here, we save the other partner, whether it be a bad wife or a bad husband, for once married they are two in one[66] (bold mine).

This is an excerpt from the Lighthouse Catholic Media CD, "*Life is Worth Living*," This and other excellent CDs are available at http://www.lighthousecatholicmedia.org/.

Appendix F - Personal Narrative from Shelby Brown

HOSPICE

Scenario #1 – Father-in-law, Death in 2013

In July of 2013, my Father in Law passed from this life into eternity. He was diagnosed with COPD years prior to his death and at the end of his life he had need of constant use of oxygen. His disease progressed to the point that the doctor's said there was nothing that could be done for him and it was a matter of time before he would die. The nursing home which he was taken to for care suggested that we bring in hospice to help with his care until his death. When the hospice nurse came to speak with us, she explained that they were there to assist the family and nursing home with the care of the patient until his death. The assistance was to include bathing, feeding, care for his bedding, and any assistance the patient needs with medications to make him more comfortable. This was on Saturday that the papers were signed for hospice assistance. We returned to Alabama due to my husband not having leave time and Sunday thru Friday seemed pretty routine with hospice administering pain medications for his comfort. During the week we talked with Dad several times a day and he talked with us and said he was being administered small doses of morphine to make him comfortable. We knew he was eating and drinking at this point because we ask about what he had eaten for his meals.

On Saturday morning, my sister-in-law called and said that Dad had taken a turn for the worse. He was no longer lucid and did not acknowledge anyone who came to see him. At this point he was not eating or drinking. We ask about them feeding him and providing liquids through IV's and was told that hospice could not do that. That they did not sustain life, just make them comfortable for their death. My husband was very concerned and talked to the nurses who said they could do nothing because he had a "Do Not Resuscitate Medical Directive" which prohibited them from giving him any kind of medical assistance to sustain his life... not even liquids through IV intervention. My husband then made the statement that if that was the case then he would get a call on Monday morning saying that his Dad was dead, because a person cannot go without water more than 3 days. At that point there was nothing that we could do.

Early on Monday morning my husband got the call that his Dad had died.

I am writing this in hopes that this will make people aware of this situation that was wrong on so many levels. The first being the "No Resuscitate Medical Directive." We were told that my Father in Law's medical directive prohibited them from doing anything to help them sustain his life. I had discussed life support with Dad on Saturday before we left Missouri and he said he did not want any artificial life support i.e. breathing tubes, or CPR which is what we all thought the medical directive addressed. Neither he, nor our family was aware that this medical directive meant that he would not be provided with liquids or food through IV's. When he was given a short time to live and hospice took control of his care, the medical directive meant he would not get life sustaining care such as food or liquids through IV's just the assistance of comfort until he died.

The second being the administration of morphine on a continual basis. Dad was given morphine in continual increasing doses until he no longer could communicate that he wanted food or drink. To my knowledge he did not request pain medications for comfort. On Saturday he was no longer having any communication about food or drink. He had been in a constant state of sleep not acknowledging anyone since Friday afternoon. My question would be.....had he not been given the continual doses of morphine would he still have been eating and drinking? Did he die from COPD or did he die from no food or water?

Dad has passed on to his eternal rest and regardless of the "could haves" or "should haves" nothing can change the result. I will ask this question… was he cheated out of the spiritual death experiences through the death process because of the administration of morphine through hospice?

Scenario #2 – Father, a death several years earlier

My father died 25 years ago from lung cancer and he also was give hospice assistance. The assistance then was so different than with my father-in-law. My father was not given any pain medications unless he ask for them. My father did not ask for pain medication so he was lucid the entire time before his death. In his death process he talked with my brother, which had past 10 years earlier, as well as talked with his mother during his death experience. We as his family shared this spiritual experience in his death progression that we could not have experienced had he been given morphine which just made him sleep.

My final statements would be this. Make sure you know all the details of a medical directive to ensure the exact results that you want at the end of life. Also is hospice, the answer to the comfort at the end of life process. Somehow in all of these lessons learned we feel cheated and deceived.

In hopes for the enlightenment of others,

Shelby Brown[67]

Shelby Brown is a member of the Holiness Church who attended a study of Church History (*EPIC: A Journey through Church History* by Steve Weidenkopf, published by Ascension Press) with members of various faith denominations at Our Lady of the Valley Catholic Community at Redstone Arsenal, Alabama. Her father-in-law died during the course of the year of this study.

REFERENCES

Reference 1 – Artificial Nutrition & Hydration

RESPONSES TO CERTAIN QUESTIONS
OF THE UNITED STATES CONFERENCE OF CATHOLIC
BISHOPS
CONCERNING ARTIFICIAL NUTRITION AND
HYDRATION

First question: *Is the administration of food and water (whether by natural or artificial means) to a patient in a "vegetative state" morally obligatory except when they cannot be assimilated by the patient's body or cannot be administered to the patient without causing significant physical discomfort?*

Response: Yes. The administration of food and water even by artificial means is, in principle, an ordinary and proportionate means of preserving life. It is therefore obligatory to the extent to which, and for as long as, it is shown to accomplish its proper finality, which is the hydration and nourishment of the patient. In this way suffering and death by starvation and dehydration are prevented.

Second question: *When nutrition and hydration are being supplied by artificial means to a patient in a "permanent vegetative state", may they be discontinued when competent physicians judge with moral certainty that the patient will never recover consciousness?*

Response: No. A patient in a "permanent vegetative state" is a person with fundamental human dignity and must, therefore, receive ordinary and proportionate care which includes, in principle, the administration of water and food even by artificial means.

The Supreme Pontiff Benedict XVI, at the Audience granted to the undersigned Cardinal Prefect of the Congregation for the Doctrine of the Faith, approved these Responses, adopted in the Ordinary Session of the Congregation, and ordered their publication.

Rome, from the Offices of the Congregation for the Doctrine of the Faith, August 1, 2007.

William Cardinal Levada
Prefect

Angelo Amato, S.D.B.
Titular Archbishop of Sila
Secretary

Reference 2 - Euthanasia

SACRED CONGREGATION FOR THE DOCTRINE OF THE FAITH

DECLARATION ON EUTHANASIA

INTRODUCTION

The rights and values pertaining to the human person occupy an important place among the questions discussed today. In this regard, the Second Vatican Ecumenical Council solemnly reaffirmed the lofty dignity of the human person, and in a special way his or her right to life. The Council therefore condemned crimes against life "such as any type of murder, genocide, abortion, euthanasia, or willful suicide" (Pastoral Constitution *Gaudium et Spes*, no. 27). More recently, the Sacred Congregation for the Doctrine of the Faith has reminded all the faithful of Catholic teaching on procured abortion.[1] The Congregation now considers it opportune to set forth the Church's teaching on euthanasia. It is indeed true that, in this sphere of teaching, the recent Popes have explained the principles, and these retain their full force[2]; but the progress of medical science in recent years has brought to the fore new aspects of the question of euthanasia, and these aspects call for further elucidation on the ethical level. In modern society, in which even the fundamental values of human life are often called into question, cultural change exercises an influence upon the way of looking at suffering and death; moreover, medicine has increased its capacity to cure and to prolong life in particular circumstances, which sometime give rise to moral problems. Thus people living in this situation experience no little anxiety about the meaning of advanced old age and death. They also begin to wonder whether they have the right to obtain for themselves or their fellowmen an "easy death," which would shorten suffering and which seems to them more in harmony with human dignity. A number of Episcopal Conferences have raised questions on this subject with the Sacred Congregation for the Doctrine of the Faith. The Congregation, having sought the opinion of experts on the various aspects of euthanasia, now wishes to respond to the Bishops' questions with the present Declaration, in order to help them to give correct teaching to the faithful entrusted to their care, and to offer them elements for reflection that they can present to the civil authorities with regard to this very serious matter. The considerations set forth in the present document concern in the first place all those who place their faith and hope in Christ, who, through His life, death and resurrection, has given a new meaning to existence and especially to the death of the Christian, as St. Paul says: "If we live, we live to the Lord, and if we die, we die to the Lord" (*Rom.* 14:8; cf. *Phil.* 1:20). As for those who profess other religions, many will agree with us that faith in God the Creator, Provider and Lord of life - if they share this belief - confers a lofty dignity upon every human person and guarantees respect for him or her. It is hoped that this Declaration will meet with the approval of many people of good will, who, philosophical or ideological differences notwithstanding, have nevertheless a lively awareness of the rights of the human person. These rights have often, in fact, been proclaimed in recent years through declarations issued by International Congresses [3]; and since it is a question here of fundamental rights inherent in every human person, it is obviously wrong to have recourse to arguments from political pluralism or religious freedom in order to deny the universal value of those rights.

I.
THE VALUE OF HUMAN LIFE

Human life is the basis of all goods, and is the necessary source and condition of every human activity and of all society. Most people regard life as something sacred and hold that no one may dispose of it at will, but believers see in life something greater, namely, a gift of God's love, which they are called upon to preserve and make fruitful. And it is this latter consideration that gives rise to the following consequences:

1. No one can make an attempt on the life of an innocent person without opposing God's love for that person, without violating a fundamental right, and therefore without committing a crime of the utmost gravity. [4]

2. Everyone has the duty to lead his or her life in accordance with God's plan. That life is entrusted to the individual as a good that must bear fruit already here on earth, but that finds its full perfection only in eternal life.

3. Intentionally causing one's own death, or suicide, is therefore equally as wrong as murder; such an action on the part of a person is to be considered as a rejection of God's sovereignty and loving plan. Furthermore, suicide is also often a refusal of love for self, the denial of a natural instinct to live, a flight from the duties of justice and charity owed to one's neighbor, to various communities or to the whole of society - although, as is generally recognized, at times there are psychological factors present that can diminish responsibility or even completely remove it. However, one must clearly distinguish suicide from that sacrifice of one's life whereby for a higher cause, such as God's glory, the salvation of souls or the service of one's brethren, a person offers his or her own life or puts it in danger (cf. *Jn.* 15:14).

II.
EUTHANASIA

In order that the question of euthanasia can be properly dealt with, it is first necessary to define the words used. Etymologically speaking, in ancient times *Euthanasia* meant an *easy death* without severe suffering. Today one no longer thinks of this original meaning of the word, but rather of some intervention of medicine whereby the suffering of sickness or of the final agony are reduced, sometimes also with the danger of suppressing life prematurely. Ultimately, the word *Euthanasia* is used in a more particular sense to mean "mercy killing," for the purpose of putting an end to extreme suffering, or having abnormal babies, the mentally ill or the incurably sick from the prolongation, perhaps for many years of a miserable life, which could impose too heavy a burden on their families or on society. It is, therefore, necessary to state clearly in what sense the word is used in the present document. By euthanasia is understood an action or an omission which of itself or by intention causes death, in order that all suffering may in this way be eliminated. Euthanasia's terms of reference, therefore, are to be found in the intention of the will and in the methods used. It is necessary to state firmly once more that nothing and no one can in any way permit the killing of an innocent human being, whether a fetus or an embryo, an infant or an adult, an old person, or one suffering from an incurable disease, or a person who is dying. Furthermore, no one is permitted to ask for this act of killing, either for himself or herself or for another person entrusted to his or her care, nor can he or she consent to it, either explicitly or implicitly. Nor can any authority legitimately recommend or permit such an action. For it is a question of the violation of the divine law, an offense against the dignity of the human person, a crime against life, and an attack on humanity. It may happen that, by reason of prolonged and barely tolerable pain, for deeply personal or other reasons, people may be led to believe that they can legitimately ask for death or obtain it for others. Although in these cases the guilt of the individual may be reduced or completely absent, nevertheless the error of judgment into which the conscience falls, perhaps in good faith, does not change the nature of this act of killing, which will always be in itself something to be rejected. The pleas of gravely ill people who sometimes ask for death are not to be understood as implying a true desire for euthanasia; in fact, it is almost always a case of an anguished plea for help and love. What a sick person needs, besides medical care, is love, the human and supernatural warmth with which the sick person can and ought to be surrounded by all those close to him or her, parents and children, doctors and nurses.

III.
THE MEANING OF SUFFERING FOR CHRISTIANS AND THE USE OF PAINKILLERS

Death does not always come in dramatic circumstances after barely tolerable sufferings. Nor do we have to think only of extreme cases. Numerous testimonies which confirm one another lead one to the conclusion that nature itself has made provision to render more bearable at the moment of death separations that would be terribly painful to a person in full health. Hence it is that a prolonged illness, advanced old age, or a state of loneliness or neglect can bring about psychological conditions that facilitate the acceptance of death. Nevertheless the fact remains that death, often preceded or accompanied by severe and prolonged suffering, is something which naturally causes people anguish. Physical suffering is certainly an unavoidable element of the human condition; on the biological level, it constitutes a warning of which no one denies the usefulness; but, since it affects the human psychological makeup, it often exceeds its own biological usefulness and so can become so severe as to cause the desire to remove it at any cost. According to Christian teaching, however, suffering, especially suffering during the last moments of life, has a special place in God's saving plan; it is in fact a sharing in Christ's passion and a union with the redeeming sacrifice which He offered in obedience to the Father's will. Therefore, one must not be surprised if some Christians prefer to moderate their use of painkillers, in order to accept voluntarily at least a part of their sufferings and thus associate themselves in a conscious way with the sufferings of Christ crucified (cf. *Mt.* 27:34). Nevertheless it would be imprudent to impose a heroic way of acting as a general rule. On the contrary, human and Christian prudence suggest for the majority of sick people the use of medicines capable of alleviating or suppressing pain, even though these may cause as a secondary effect semi-consciousness and reduced lucidity. As for those who are not in a state to express themselves, one can reasonably presume that they wish to take these painkillers, and have them administered according to the doctor's advice. But the intensive use of painkillers is not without difficulties, because the phenomenon of habituation generally makes it necessary to increase their dosage in order to maintain their efficacy. At this point it is fitting to recall a declaration by Pius XII, which retains its full force; in answer to a group of doctors who had put the question: "Is the suppression of pain and consciousness by the use of narcotics ... permitted by religion and morality to the doctor and the patient (even at the approach of death and if one foresees that the use of narcotics will shorten life)?" the Pope said: "If no other means exist, and if, in the given circumstances, this does not prevent the carrying out of other religious and moral duties: Yes."[5] In this case, of course, death is in no way intended or sought, even if the risk of it is reasonably taken; the intention is simply to relieve pain effectively, using for this purpose painkillers available to medicine. However, painkillers that cause unconsciousness need special consideration. For a person not only has to be able to satisfy his or her moral duties and family obligations; he or she also has to prepare himself or herself with full consciousness for meeting Christ. Thus Pius XII warns: "It is not right to deprive the dying person of consciousness without a serious reason."[6]

IV.
DUE PROPORTION IN THE USE OF REMEDIES

Today it is very important to protect, at the moment of death, both the dignity of the human person and the Christian concept of life, against a technological attitude that threatens to become an abuse. Thus some people speak of a "right to die," which is an expression that does not mean the right to procure death either by one's own hand or by means of someone else, as one pleases, but rather the right to die peacefully with human and Christian dignity. From this point of view, the use of therapeutic means can sometimes pose problems. In numerous cases, the complexity of the situation can be such as to cause doubts about the way ethical principles should be applied. In the final analysis, it pertains to the conscience either of the sick person, or of those qualified to speak in the sick person's name, or of the doctors, to decide, in the light of moral obligations and of the various aspects of the case. Everyone has the duty to care for his or he own health or to seek such care from others. Those whose task it is to care for the sick must do so conscientiously and administer the remedies that seem necessary or useful. However, is it necessary in all circumstances to have recourse to all possible remedies? In the past, moralists replied that one is never obliged to use "extraordinary" means. This reply, which as a principle still holds good, is perhaps less clear today, by reason of the imprecision of the term and the rapid progress made in the treatment of sickness. Thus some people prefer to speak of "proportionate" and "disproportionate" means. In any case, it will be possible to make a correct judgment as to the means by studying the type of treatment to be used, its degree of complexity or risk, its cost and the possibilities of using it, and comparing these elements with the result that can be expected, taking into account the state of the sick person and his or her physical and moral resources. In order to facilitate the application of these general principles, the following clarifications can be added: - If there are no other sufficient remedies, it is permitted, with the patient's consent, to have recourse to the means provided by the most advanced medical techniques, even if these means are still at the experimental stage and are not without a certain risk. By accepting them, the patient can even show generosity in the service of humanity. - It is also permitted, with the patient's consent, to interrupt these means, where the results fall short of expectations. But for such a decision to be made, account will have to be taken of the reasonable wishes of the patient and the patient's family, as also of the advice of the doctors who are specially competent in the matter. The latter may in particular judge that the investment in instruments and personnel is disproportionate to the results foreseen; they may also judge that the techniques applied impose on the patient strain or suffering out of proportion with the benefits which he or she may gain from such techniques. - It is also permissible to make do with the normal means that medicine can offer. Therefore one cannot impose on anyone the obligation to have recourse to a technique which is already in use but which carries a risk or is burdensome. Such a refusal is not the equivalent of suicide; on the contrary, it should be considered as an acceptance of the human condition, or a wish to avoid the application of a medical procedure disproportionate to the results that can be expected, or a desire not to impose excessive expense on the family or the community. - When inevitable death is imminent in spite of the means used, it is permitted in conscience to take the decision to refuse forms of treatment that would only secure a precarious and burdensome prolongation of life, so long as the normal care due to the sick person in similar cases is not interrupted. In such circumstances the doctor has no reason to reproach himself with failing to help the person in danger.

CONCLUSION

The norms contained in the present Declaration are inspired by a profound desire to service people in accordance with the plan of the Creator. Life is a gift of God, and on the other hand death is unavoidable; it is necessary, therefore, that we, without in any way hastening the hour of death, should be able to accept it with full responsibility and dignity. It is true that death marks the end of our earthly existence, but at the same time it opens the door to immortal life. Therefore, all must prepare themselves for this event in the light of human values, and Christians even more so in the light of faith. As for those who work in the medical profession, they ought to neglect no means of making all their skill available to the sick and dying; but they should also remember how much more necessary it is to provide them with the comfort of boundless kindness and heartfelt charity. Such service to people is also service to Christ the Lord, who said: "As you did it to one of the least of these my brethren, you did it to me" (*Mt.* 25:40).

At the audience granted prefect, His Holiness Pope John Paul II approved this declaration, adopted at the ordinary meeting of the Sacred Congregation for the Doctrine of the Faith, and ordered its publication.

Rome, the Sacred Congregation for the Doctrine of the Faith, May 5, 1980.

Franjo Cardinal Seper
Prefect

Jerome Hamer, O.P.
Tit. Archbishop of Lorium
Secretary

FOOTNOTES

[1] DECLARATION ON PROCURED ABORTION, November 18, 1974: AAS 66 (1974), pp. 730-747.

[2] Pius XII, ADDRESS TO THOSE ATTENDING THE CONGRESS OF THE INTERNATIONAL UNION OF CATHOLIC WOMEN'S LEAGUES, September 11, 1947: AAS 39 (1947), p. 483; ADDRESS TO THE ITALIAN CATHOLIC UNION OF MIDWIVES, October 29, 1951: AAS 43 (1951), pp. 835-854; SPEECH TO THE MEMBERS OF THE INTERNATIONAL OFFICE OF MILITARY MEDICINE DOCUMENTATION, October 19, 1953: AAS 45 (1953), pp. 744-754; ADDRESS TO THOSE TAKING PART IN THE IXth CONGRESS OF THE ITALIAN ANAESTHESIOLOGICAL SOCIETY, February 24, 1957: AAS 49 (1957), p. 146; cf. also ADDRESS ON "REANIMATION," November 24, 1957: AAS 49 (1957), pp. 1027-1033; Paul VI, ADDRESS TO THE MEMBERS OF THE UNITED NATIONAL SPECIAL COMMITTEE ON APARTHEID, May 22, 1974: AAS 66 (1974), p. 346; John Paul II: ADDRESS TO THE BISHOPS OF THE UNITED STATES OF AMERICA, October 5, 1979: AAS 71 (1979), p. 1225.

[3] One thinks especially of Recommendation 779 (1976) on the rights of the sick and dying, of the Parliamentary Assembly of the Council of Europe at its XXVIIth Ordinary Session; cf. Sipeca, no. 1, March 1977, pp. 14-15.

[4] We leave aside completely the problems of the death penalty and of war, which involve specific considerations that do not concern the present subject.

[5] Pius XII, ADDRESS of February 24, 1957: AAS 49 (1957), p. 147.

[6] Pius XII, Ibid., p. 145; cf. ADDRESS of September 9, 1958: AAS 50 (1958), p. 694.

Reference 3 – Papal Documents

» Caritas in Veritate (Charity in Truth), Encyclical, Pope Benedict XVI, 2009 (http://w2.vatican.va/content/benedict-xvi/en/encyclicals/documents/hf_ben-xvi_enc_20090629_caritas-in-veritate.html)

» Casti Connubii (On Christian Marriage), Encyclical, Pope Pius XI, 1930 (http://w2.vatican.va/content/pius-xi/en/encyclicals/documents/hf_p-xi_enc_31121930_casti-connubii.html)

» Evangelium Vitae (Gospel of Life), Encyclical, Pope John Paul II, 1995 (http://w2.vatican.va/content/john-paul-ii/en/encyclicals/documents/hf_jp-ii_enc_25031995_evangelium-vitae.html)

» Familiaris Consortio (On the Role of the Christian Family in the Modern World), Apostolic Exhortation, Pope St. John Paul II, 1981 (http://w2.vatican.va/content/john-paul-ii/en/apost_exhortations/documents/hf_jp-ii_exh_19811122_familiaris-consortio.html)

» Gratissimam Sane (Letter to Families) promulgated by Pope St. John Paul II, 1994 (http://w2.vatican.va/content/john-paul-ii/en/letters/1994/documents/hf_jp-ii_let_02021994_families.html)

» Humane Vitae (On the Regulation of Birth), Encyclical, Pope Paul VI, 1968 (http://w2.vatican.va/content/paul-vi/en/encyclicals/documents/hf_p-vi_enc_25071968_humanae-vitae.html)

» Salvifici Doloris (On the Meaning of Christian Suffering), Encyclical, Pope John Paul II, 1984 (http://w2.vatican.va/content/john-paul-ii/en/apost_letters/1984 /documents/hf_jpii_apl_11021984_salvifici-doloris.html)

» Veritatis Splendor (Splendor of Truth), Encyclical, Pope John Paul II, 1993 (http://w2.vatican.va/content/john-paul-ii/en/encyclicals/documents/hf_jp-ii_enc_06081993_veritatis-splendor.html)

Reference 4 – Congregation for the Doctrine of the Faith (CDF) Documents

» Responses to Certain Questions of the USCCB Concerning Artificial Nutrition and Hydration, CDF, 2007 (http://www.vatican.va/roman_curia/congregations/cfaith/docum ents/rc_con_cfaith_doc_20070801_risposte-usa_en.html)

» Dignitas Personae (Instruction on Certain Bioethical Questions), CDF, 2008 (http://www.vatican.va/roman_curia/congregations/cfaith/docum ents/rc_con_cfaith_doc_20081208_dignitas-personae_en.html)

» Clarification on Procured Abortions, CDF, 2009 (http://www.vatican.va/roman_curia/congregations/cfaith/docum ents/rc_con_cfaith_doc_20090711_aborto-procurato_en.html)

» Responses to Questions Proposed Concerning "Uterine Isolation" and Related Matters, CDF, 1993 (http://www.vatican.va/roman_curia/congregations/cfaith/docum ents/rc_con_cfaith_doc_31071994_uterine-isolation_en.html)

» The Moral Norm of "Humane Vitae" and Pastoral Duty, CDF, 1989 (http://www.vatican.va/roman_curia/congregations/cfaith/docum ents/rc_con_cfaith_doc_19890216_norma-morale_en.html)

» Donum Vitae (Instructions on Respect for Human Life in its Origin and on the Dignity of Procreation), CDF, 1987 (www.vatican.va/roman_curia/congregations/cfaith/documents/rc _con_cfaith_doc_19870222_respect-for-human-life_en.html)

» Iura et bona (Declaration on Euthanasia), (CDF), 1980 (http://www.vatican.va/roman_curia/congregations/cfaith/docum ents/rc_con_cfaith_doc_19800505_euthanasia_en.html)

» Persona Humana (Declaration on Certain Questions Concerning Sexual Ethics), CDF, 1975 (http://www.vatican.va/roman_curia/congregations/cfaith/docum ents/rc_con_cfaith_doc_19751229_persona-humana_en.html)

» Responses to Questions Concerning Sterilization in Catholic Hospitals, CDF, 1975 (http://www.vatican.va/roman_curia/ congregations/cfaith/documents/rc_con_cfaith_doc_19750313_q uaecumque-sterilizatio_en.html)

» Declaration on Procured Abortions, CDF, 1974 (http://www.vatican.va/roman_curia/congregations/cfaith/docum ents/rc_con_cfaith_doc_19741118_declaration-abortion_en.html)

» Letter to the Bishop of Cleveland regarding the Questions Proposed on the Cremation of Fetuses and Members of the Human Body, CDF, 1967 (http://www.vatican.va/roman_curia/congregations/cfaith/docum ents/rc_con_cfaith_doc_19670307_dubia-prop-foetus_en.html)

Reference 5 – Free Consultation on Bioethical Issues

Free Consultation Services on Bioethical Issues

Available through the National Catholic Bioethics Center-NCBC

The NCBC offers a free consultation service, by a credentialed bioethicist, who can share the Catholic principles for addressing an ethical dilemma involving health care or the life sciences. If the question is time-sensitive concerning such a matter that cannot wait until regular business hours, call: **(215) 877-2660, 24 hours/day, 7 days/week.** Follow the prompts to leave a message and an ethicist will be paged and respond to the call as soon as possible.

If the question is not related to a time sensitive matter call the same number during regular business hours 9am – 5pm Eastern Time or use the online Consultation Request Form at www.ncbcenter.org Select the "Consultation" tab and "Submit a Request" in the drop down menu.

NOTE: The National Catholic Bioethics Center (Center) is a non-profit research and educational institute committed to applying the moral teachings of the Catholic Church to ethical issues arising in health care and the life sciences. The Center provides consultations to institutions and individuals seeking its opinion on the appropriate application of Catholic moral teachings to these ethical issues.

Neither the Center's moral analyses nor any other project of the Center should be construed as an attempt to offer or render a legal or medical opinion or otherwise to engage in the practice of law or medicine, or other health care disciplines.

Note from the author: – The above is provided to be of assistance to individuals dealing with difficult ethical issues. Providing this reference should in no way be construed as the NCBC support for this book which was not submitted for their review. The NCBC also provides *A Catholic Guide to End of Life Decisions* available for purchase at a minimal fee on their website www.ncbcenter.org under the "Publications" tab.

ENDNOTES

[1] General Carl von Clausewitz,*On War. https://edcat.uni-muenster.de/.../Clausewitz%20%22On%20War%22.pdf* (accessed October 25, 2014), Section 24, 22.

[2] Peter Kreeft, *Making Sense Out of Suffering* (Cincinnati: St. Anthony Messenger Press, 1986), 3.

[3] Dom Hubert van Zeller, *Suffering: The Catholic Answer.* (Manchester, NH: Sophia Institute, 2002), 55-56.

[4] Francesco Giammarile, Thomas Mognetti, I. Resche, *Bone pain palliation with strontium-89 in cancer patients with bone metastasis*. Quarterly Journal of Nuclear Medicine, 2001 Mar, 45(1), 78-83.

[5] George Isajiw, Medical education in the shadows of 'stealth euthanasia' among Catholics: Are we fighting secularism or heresy? *The Linacre Quarterly*, 82 (3) (August 2015); 211-212.

[6] Venerable Archbishop J. Fulton Sheen, *Calvary and the Mass: The Consecration* in Sancta Missa, (http://www.sanctamissa.org/en/resources/books/calvary/the-consecration.html (accessed 23Oct2015), 2010.

[7] IASP, http://www.iasp-pain.org/Taxonomy?navItemNumber=576#Pain (accessed October 23, 2014).

[8] Margo McCaffery, *Nursing Practice Theories Related to Cognition, Bodily Pain and Man-Environment Interactions* (Los Angeles: UCLA, 1968), 95.

[9] Eric Cassell, "The Relationship between Pain and Suffering," in *Advances in Pain Research and Therapy,* ed. C. Stratton Hill Jr. and William S. Fields (New York: Raven Press Ltd, 1989), 63.

[10] Aaron Kheriaty, *The Catholic Guide to Depression* (Manchester, NH: Sophia Institute Press, 2012), 103.

[11] Saint Aurelius Augustine, *Confessions* III, VII, 12 (Chicago: Encyclopedia Britannica, Inc, 1984), 16.

[12] Ibid., Book I, I, 1.

[13] Kreeft, *Making Sense of Suffering*, 24.

[14] Sister Catherine Joseph Droste, Madelyn Winstead and Terry Polakovic, *Setting the World Ablaze: Saint Catherine of Siena* (Denver: ENDOW, 2014), 140-41.

[15] Joseph Ratzinger, *Jesus of Nazareth* (New York: Doubleday, 2007), 162.

[16] Mother M. Angelica, *The Healing Power of Suffering (*Birmingham, Alabama: EWTN, 1977), 21.

[17] Fr. John A. Hardon, *God the Author of Nature and the Supernatural Part Two: Creation as a Divine Fact; Section Two: Supernatural Anthropology,* http://www.therealpresence.org/archives/God/God_013.htm, (accessed 9Dec2014), 2000.

[18]Ibid.

[19] Zeller, *Suffering,* 96.

[20] Peter Kreeft, *Making Sense of Suffering,* 177.

[21] Edward Leen, *Why the Cross?* (Rochelle, NY: Scepter, 1938), 282.

[22] Zeller, *Suffering,* 96.

[23] John A. Kane, *How to Make a Good Confession* (Manchester: New Hampshire, Sophia Institute, 2001), 24.

[24] Russell Shaw, *Does Suffering Make Sense?* (New York: Scepter Publishers, 1975), 89.

[25] Leen, *Why the Cross?* 150.

[26] Zeller, *Suffering: The Catholic Answer,* 24.

[27] Ibid., 153.

[28] Kreeft, *Making Sense out of Suffering,* 169.

[29] Zeller, *Suffering: The Catholic Answer,* 14-15.

[30] Leen, *Why the Cross?,* 87.

[31] Rod Dreher, *How Dante Can Save Your Life: The Life-Changing Wisdom of History's Greatest Poem* (New York: Regan Arts, 2015), 284.

[32] Peter Kreeft, *Making Sense of Suffering,* 138.

[33] Darrel Philip Kaiser, *Widower: Our Story of God's Grace, Mercy and Blessings* (Huntsville, AL: Green Mountain, 2013), 82-89.

[34] Mother Angelica, *The Healing Power of Suffering,* 15.

[35] Rod Dreher, *How Dante Can Save Your Life,* 248.

[36] Mother Angelica, *The Healing Power of Suffering,* 18.

[37]Scott Hahn & Curtis Mitch, In *The Ignatius Study Bible,* 2ed, (San Francisco: Ignatius Press, 2010), 366.

[38] Cesar Alejandro Mora Paz, *Colossians.* In *The International Bible Commentary* ed. William R. Farmer (Collegeville, MN: Liturgical Press, 1998), 1703.

[39] Scott Hahn & Curtis Mitch, *Ignatius Study Bible,* 366.

[40] St. Alphonsus, *Thoughts on the Passion* in *The Navarre Bible: The Letters of Saint Paul* (New York: Scepter, 2008), 474.

[41] Mother Angelica, *The Healing Power of Suffering,* 18.

[42] Ibid., 19.

[43] Zeller, *Suffering: The Catholic Answer*, 97.

[44] Hahn & Mitch, In *Ignatius Catholic Study Bible,* 358.

[45] Zeller, *Suffering: The Catholic Answer*, 41.

[46] Dreher, *How Dante Can Save Your Life*, 202.

[47] Mother Angelica, *The Healing Power of Suffering,* 16.

[48] Ibid., 18.

[49] Ibid., 16.

[50] Zeller, *Suffering: The Catholic Answer,* 98.

[51] Ibid., 41.

[52] Ibid., 64-65.

[53] St. Rose of Lima. In *The Liturgy of the Hours: IV,* (New York: Catholic Book Publishing, 1975), 1342-43.

[54] Mother Teresa. "Address at the Cathedral of St. Mary of the Assumption," San Francisco (audiocassette), 1982.

[55] Betty Bland, Personal Communication, Huntsville, AL, 2014.

[56] St. Paul of the Cross. *Liturgy of the Hours, IV,* (New York: Catholic Book Publishing, 1975), 1505-06.

[57] Joan Carroll Cruz, *Saints for the Sick* (Charlotte, NC: TAN Books, 2010), 216.

[58] Ibid., 217.

[59] Leen, *Why the Cross?*, 240.

[60] Ibid., 240.

[61] Sharon van der Sloot, *Salvifici Doloris: A Study Guide* (Denver: ENDOW, 2008), 76.

[62] Jason Evert, *Parenting for Purity,* CD-ROM (Lighthouse Catholic Media, 2013).

[63] Mother Teresa. Address at the Cathedral of St. Mary of the Assumption, San Francisco (audiocassette), 1982.

[64] Jeremiah Denton, When Hell was in Session (Washington, D.C., WorldNetDaily, 1998), 125.

[65] Jeremiah Denton, *Walking through the Valley of the Shadow of Death,* CD-ROM (Grand Rapids, MI: Lighthouse Catholic Media, 2014).

[66] Archbishop Fulton Sheen, *The Problem of Love* in *Life is Worthy Living,* CD-ROM (Grand Rapids, MI: Lighthouse Catholic Media, 2014).

[67] Shelby Brown, Personal Communication, (Huntsville, AL, 2013).

Printed in Great Britain
by Amazon

45705808R00080